THE VOICES OF ROMANCE

The Voices of Romance
Studies in Dialogue and Character

Ann Dobyns

DELAWARE

Newark: University of Delaware Press
London and Toronto: Associated University Presses

Associated University Presses
440 Forsgate Drive
Cranbury, NJ 08512

Associated University Presses
25 Sicilian Avenue
London WC1A 2QH, England

Associated University Presses
P.O. Box 488, Port Credit
Mississauga, Ontario
Canada L5G 4M2

The paper used in this publication meets the requirements
of the American National Standard for Permanence of Paper
for Printed Library Materials Z39.48–1984.

Library of Congress Cataloging-in-Publication Data

Dobyns, Ann, 1946–
    The voices of romance: studies in dialogue and character/Ann
Dobyns.
        p.   cm.
    Bibliography: p.
    Includes index.
    ISBN 0-87413-351-3 (alk. paper)
    1. English literature—History and criticism.   2. Romances,
English—History and criticism.   3. Characters and characteristics
in literature.   4. Malory, Thomas, Sir, 15th cent. Morte d'Arthur.
5. Sidney, Philip, Sir, 1554–1586.   Arcadia.   6. Brontë, Emily,
1818–1848. Wuthering heights.   7. Arthurian romances—History and
criticism.   8. Dialogue.   I. Title.
PR408.R7D64   1989
820'.9'26—dc19   88-40342
                                                                    CIP

For my son, Jeff Mount,
and in memory of my father, Donald Keith Dobyns

Contents

Preface

This book grew out of my interest in stylized literature, initially English romances written in the later Middle Ages. Unlike the French romances on which they are based, English medieval romances are overtly conventional. They exhibit simplified plot structures and, in addition, show little evidence of such embellishments as the characters' thoughts or elaborate descriptions of scenes or the actors, such as are typical of their sources. These more simplified versions of familiar tales draw attention to the structures of their stories as structure. Stripped of their sources' detail and complexity of plot, their mythic level stands out, the forms of their designs brought into sharp relief. Observing the designs of these romances, one notices immediately that rather than progressing in an apparently logical manner—as one would expect in a story that ostensibly imitates a potential experience—these tales progress by means of coincidence, repetition, and elaboration. Their dominant structural characteristic is episodic; thus, the story is a chain of loosely connected adventures. Concurrently, the elements of the structure are subservient to the episode and not necessarily consistent throughout the work. Characters, for example, exhibit traits depending on the demands of the context rather than being determined by any idea of a coherent individual. In one episode a character may exhibit a particular set of characteristics, then may appear quite different when a new episode requires somewhat contradictory traits. Characters are thus more explicitly a part of the pattern of the text rather than the focus of attention, as they frequently are in mimetic fiction. Although such textual characteristics are more observable in Middle English romances with their simplified form, these same features distinguish their French sources (despite the added details). In fact, they characterize romances in general, from Spenser's *Fairie Queene* to the contemporary drugstore romances.

The seminal studies of this phenomenon are, of course, Northrop Frye's structural analyses of romance—in his *Anatomy of Criticism*, *A Natural Perspective*, and *The Secular Scripture*. In each work, Frye is interested in the conventions governing the genre. Romance,

Frye argues repeatedly, is structurally different from mimetic fiction. One way to explain the difference is by describing mimetic fiction as that in which the logic of the narrative line controls the structure and romance as that in which an idea or mood controls the structure. Frye calls the narrative structure of mimetic fiction, with its sense of logical progression, horizontal, whereas he identifies romance, with its episodic pattern, as vertical. Thus, mimetic fiction seems to be syllogistic and romance thematic. In order to demonstrate its thematic unity expressed in the pattern of the text, romance shows the contours of its narrative. The genre is thus governed by an aesthetic principle different from that of mimetic fiction. Frye compares this difference to that seen between representational and abstract art—like the works of abstract art, romances make prominent the spatial rather than the psychological structure of the stories they tell.

In his most recent book on romance, Frye not only observes the distinction between the genres but also urges critics "to learn to look at romances, with all their nonrepresentational plots and characters, equally on their own terms."[1] Unlike art critics who have done justice to abstract art, however, all too often critics of fiction have neglected the study of conventions of abstract form, particularly in studies of romance. Frye's book is an attempt to raise the study of romance to a more sophisticated level of analysis, and indeed his study does so. However, although he devotes an entire chapter of his study to a discussion of the ways romance heroes and heroines represent the ritualized action of romance (because he is concerned with all the elements of romance), Frye does not discuss specific techniques of characterization. In order to consider romance with the same care and respect as realism, we need to go beyond Frye and examine the techiques of romance characterization.

The dominant theory of the ways romance writers create characters is that they use types or caricatures, generally neglect verisimilitude of detail, and rarely develop distinct differentiated characters. In fact, assuming that romance characters are narrowly defined and idealized, few critics have examined the techniques writers of these works use to develop their characters. However, the observations that romance characters are abstract or conventional does not logically justify the conclusions that their authors rarely develop distinct or differentiated characters. Indeed, conventional characters do not inherently lack complexity simply because they represent abstract ideas or ideals.

Instead of accepting the standard premise, I suggest entertaining an alternate hypothesis. If we assume that romance is a thematic genre (as most theorists of romance assume), one controlling question for any study of romance must be: In what ways do authors explore or develop their themes? In addition to setting and narrative structure, certainly characters, as ideas or ideals, must in some way contribute to the creation of theme. One way they may do so is by drawing the reader's attention to the work's central ideas by representing opposing forces of good and evil, for example. This technique is widely recognized by critics who have written about romance. Characters representing abstract forces are typically one-dimensional, pure, uncomplicated emblems. A more subtle way, however, that writers may demonstrate ideas central to their works is by making multifaceted characters who illustrate, within their portraits, the complexity of the ideas the writer presents. In order to exemplify various qualities of the central idea, characters must have some notable, distinct qualities themselves.

One of the dimensions writers add, when they go beyond the mere recitation of plot lines, is dialogue between the agents of the action. This case occurs whether the writer is creating episodic or causal actions. In representational fiction, the words characters speak give the reader insight into the kind of potential person represented, which frequently is the major focus of the text. As W. J. Harvey has observed, great novels exist to reveal and explore the people who inhabit them. Romance, however, has a different purpose. If the characters represent ideas rather than potential persons, then their speeches must also function quite differently than do the words spoken by characters in mimetic fiction.

My study of techniques of romance characterization begins with the hypothesis that in order to illustrate the central ideas of their romances, writers may use speech characteristics to develop distinct and complex characters without making them imitative of a potential lived experience. Rather, the agents constructed through the words assigned represent some central idea the writer wishes to draw to the reader's attention as being significant to the thematic concern of the work. One way that writers accomplish this task is by distinguishing the speech patterns between characters of the same type, thus producing a complexity of characterization distinct from that of more representational fiction.

To illustrate this different kind of characterization, I compare parallel characters from three romances: Thomas Malory's *Le Morte Darthur*, Philip Sidney's *New Arcadia*, and Emily Brontë's *Wuthering Heights*. I have chosen these three because each represents the apex of a historical romance tradition: *Le Morte Darthur* of the Middle English prose romance, the *New Arcadia* of the English Renaissance prose romance, and *Wuthering Heights* of the eighteenth-century, early nineteenth-century gothic romance. As such, the three works represent romance in three different centuries and thus offer the possibility of a historical perspective of characterization in romance. In addition, each work has been the focus of critical controversies directly related to the question of characterization. Finally, each work contains a pair of characters whom the authors have placed in parallel situations: in *Le Morte Darthur*, Guinevere and Isode; in the *New Arcadia*, the princesses and sisters Pamela and Philoclea; in *Wuthering Heights*, Catherine Earnshaw Linton and her daughter Cathy. These parallels in type and role present the opportunity to isolate and compare the similarities and differences in typed characters, and thus to examine complex nonmimetic constructs.

Analyzing the discourse of these pairs, I examine the character traits of these parallel characters as expressed by their manner of speaking and, in addition, illustrate ways these romance writers differentiate similar characters while maintaining their typicality. By doing so, I explore the rhetorical function created by the tension between type and individual. In each case, my analysis is based on a close look at sentences and units of discourse—their diction, grammatical components, beginning and closing form, syntax, and structure and length—in an attempt to establish a precise description of the speaking style of each character. I then compare the descriptions of the parallel characters in general and in different as well as similar speaking situations.

Each work requires a slightly different approach. Representing a highly conventionalized genre, Malory's *Le Morte Darthur* demands a consideration of verbal formulas as well as conventions of diction, syntax, and formal structure of speeches. Sidney wrote the *New Arcadia* in a genre quite different from *Le Morte Darthur*'s; Sidney relied on a sophisticated knowledge of the schemes and tropes of classical rhetoric. Consequently, his work benefits from a close examination of his use of rhetorical figures. *Wuthering Heights*, written after the establishment of the novel, is more amenable to an evaluation of the way the structure of longer speeches, the diction, and grammatical components imitate the nature of the empirical world.

The analysis that follows suggests that in romance as well as mimetic fiction, character development is important in creating unity. Further, character in romance is likewise established through the subtleties of dialogue. Finally, the study of romance may benefit from the sorts of literary stylistic analyses that attend to the connections between a writer's rhetorical choices and the world offered by that writer's text.

Acknowledgments

Many collegues and friends assisted me in preparing this book, and I am grateful for their help. I am indebted first to Stanley B. Greenfield and James L. Boren for their kind and wise direction of this project when it began as a dissertation. For encouragement and criticism, I owe thanks to Katherine Burkman, Kathleen Dubs, David Frantz, Susan Hawkins, John Gage, Lisa Kiser, James Phelan, Arnold Shapiro, Christian Zacher, and particularly Andrea Hammer at Associated University Presses. I am also grateful to Oxford University Press for permission to quote extensively from *The Works of Sir Thomas Malory*, 2d ed., edited by Eugène Vinaver, 1971; to Cambridge University Press for permission to quote extensively from *The Prose Works of Sir Philip Sidney*, edited by Albert Feuillerat, 1965; and to W. W. Norton and Company for permission to quote extensively from *Wuthering Heights: An Authoritative Text with Essays in Criticism*, 2d ed., edited by William M. Sale, Jr., 1972. Chapter 2 appeared in somewhat different form in *Texas Studies in Literature and Language*, vol. 28, no. 4, winter 1986 and a version of chapter 3 in *Style*, vol. 20, no. 2, summer 1986. Time to revise the manuscript came from a Special Research Assignment from the College of Humanities at the Ohio State University. Finally, I want to thank my family for their continuing love and support: my mother, Kathleen Dobyns, my children, Jeff and Sarah, and especially my husband, Neil Bania.

THE VOICES OF ROMANCE

1
Characterization in Romance

The term *romance* has been interpreted in many different ways in the history of Anglo-American literature. Often used to label any nonhistorical account, and thus embracing all forms of fiction, romance has come to be associated with works ruled by the imagination rather than reason. Despite differences in interpretation, Clara Reeve's distinction, in her 1785 study of fiction, seems to have remained the dominant general definition. "The Novel," she observed, "is a picture of real life and manners, and of the time in which it is written. The Romance, in lofty and elevated language, describes what never happened nor is likely to happen." Despite the acceptance of this general definition, differences have existed and still remain in the application of the generic term. In fact, in a recent study of romance in American literature, Michael Davitt Bell notes the various interpretations of the term and specifically distinguishes between what he calls the radical and conservative positions. According to the radical definition, when one labels a work a romance, it is in response to the "lack of integration between the actual and imaginary," the criterion Henry James uses to characterize romances. By this definition, the romance is engaged in an act of play, in creating an experience that denies the laws of reason. In contrast, the conservative definition, represented in American literary history by Nathaniel Hawthorne, is a more aesthetic one, as Bell indicates. According to Hawthorne, a romance is a work in which the writer employs imaginative elements in order to explore a human issue.[1]

The difference between these two views is in emphasis as well as specific subject matter. The radical definition embraces all works having fantasy as their subject matter, despite the writer's purpose in choosing such materials. The conservative definition, conversely, focuses on any work using "nonmimetic" elements to illustrate an idea—in Hawthorne's view, a moral position; a looser reading of his definition, however, would include the presentation or exploration of any first principle. If the subject matter is fantastic, the other-worldly quality allows the writer to focus on ideas without the constraints of plausibility. Rather than attempting to conform to reality, then, romance explicitly and often self-consciously conforms to its own laws,[2] ones determined by the demands of a controlling idea.

Because I am interested in examining the literary techniques writers consciously work with when they write romance, I begin with the conservative or aesthetic position. Thus, the narrow definition of romance is any work whose central purpose is the illustration of an idea rather than the imitation of a potential real action. In other words, romance functions as an explicitly rhetorical rather than imitative genre. To put it in Aristotelian terms, in romance the idea becomes the persuasive purpose and the manner of presentation its means of persuasion. Although this definition may be an artificially narrow one, it allows me to isolate and study characters who function nonmimetically as expressions of ideas. Before doing so, however, I will explore the implications of a definition of romance as a rhetorical genre.

The Rhetoric of Romance

At the end of the nineteenth century, W. P. Ker defined the medieval romance as the kind of story in which life was portrayed "in a conventional or abstract manner," in which characters were "obviously breathed upon by the master of the show to convey his own ideas."[3] Today, nearly a century later, one commonly held critical view of romance follows Ker's evaluation closely. According to critics from Ker to Northrop Frye, the world of romance is one of ideas, and the reader generally feels the guiding hand of the author choosing fictional elements that best express the logic of the work's central idea.[4] As such, romances typically have a formal unity different from that of the novel. Because the romancer's interest is in the idea—not in the action for itself—the reader never has the sense of a word, personality, or situation drawing attention from the controlling form. Rather, these elements draw attention to themselves as representatives or reflections of the idea. To achieve this aesthetic distance, the romancer creates a schism between the meaning of words and images, and their concrete nature as objects. The conscious patterning, foregrounding the spatial quality of the text, may be created through such means as alliteration, pronounced and noticeable rhythm, unexpected tropes, striking speech conventions, startling or fantastic descriptions, or the repetition of a word or phrase. Whatever the means, the effect is one in which the central idea controls the framework for its presentation.

Because its purpose is so different from the novel, we might then compare romance with allegory, the other end of the fictional spectrum with which romance shares many characteristics. Like allegory, romance illustrates an idea. Indeed, without the absolute consistency of scenes and characters representing specific moral qualities, as is characteristic of pure allegory, all details of a romance—the plot, language, actions, characters, setting, and symbols—likewise cohere to form a consistent whole. In romance, however, the writer plays with conventions or stock elements, adding complexity to develop the idea rather than simply labeling and personifying abstract concepts. The romancer may, for instance, repeat motifs or significant words or phrases, create mirror characters, set parallel chapters, or pause to describe in detail various facets of an emblem—all to demonstrate the ways in which the interaction of these details illustrates the central principle of the work. Despite the difference in complexity, the similarities between the two genres become more obvious when writers of allegory add details to their abstract concepts in an attempt to develop the idea further. When they do so, these authors resemble the writers of romance. Thus, works such as Bunyan's *Pilgrim's Progress* sometimes lean toward romance when the writer lingers to multiply the details of a scene or episode with catalogs, descriptions, or extended adventures, as long as the reason for doing so appears to be the illustration of the emblematic nature of the episode or the object described rather than simply a momentary interest in the action or character at hand.[5]

This emblematic quality of romance suggests the analogy to abstract or symbolic art that Northrop Frye observes. Like abstract art, romances rely less on realistic rendering than on the symbolic placement of the aspects of a mosaic emblem. These aspects develop the romancer's idea through their spatial arrangement. Like the symbolic artist, the romancer creates tonal relationships among the various components on the literary canvas. The painter works with such details as brush stroke, light, color, and space, whereas the writer of romance may repeat words, phrases, descriptions, or motifs to evoke the symbolic relationships.

This rhetorical aspect of romance has given writers the opportunity to explore ideas without the constraints of plausibility or logical motivation. Discussing his choice of the romance genre for his fictional works, for example, Nathaniel Hawthorne pointed precisely to the greater latitude offered by the genre. In his introduction to

The House of Seven Gables, Hawthorne distinguished works of romance from novels by explaining that although the novel aims to achieve fidelity with human experience, romances are subject to the laws of truth in the human heart. Consequently, the writer of a romance "may so manage his atmospherical medium as to bring out or mellow the lights and deepen and enrich the shadows of the picture,"[6] rather than being concerned with verisimilitude. The reader can see Hawthorne's attempts to manage his medium in all his works, but perhaps never more clearly than in *The Scarlet Letter*, which will serve well as an illustration of the the rhetorical nature of romance.

The controlling idea of *The Scarlet Letter* is difficult to pin down, however. As illustrations of principles, or the conflict of principles, romances are not easily summarized. Although no great agreement exists as to the conclusions Hawthorne wished the reader to draw, there has been widespread accord concerning Hawthorne's general concern and the remarkable control of the narrative techniques he manipulates to his ends. To say that Hawthorne's work explores the nature of sin, of the suffering of the human heart, is not to go very far in explaining the complexity of the romance (particularly because such a statement does not distinguish it from Hawthorne's other works), but it is at least a beginning.[7] The action of the book chronicles this exploration of the nature of sin (or what society perceives as sin) and its effects both on the individuals involved and the community that judges the sinners. To illustrate the fable, Hawthorne manages his atmospheric medium deftly, and as a result the book's various elements both reflect and concentrate the tonal inflection. The action, for example, focuses entirely on the effects of the adulterous act, from the brief first chapter's intimation of the occurrence of the "sin" and the general community's response to it, through the gradual changes in the central participants involved with the act, and finally to their ultimate earthly destiny. To intensify these changes, Hawthorne creates a symbolic design, as F. O. Matthiessen has observed, which becomes emblematic of the controlling symbol. The three scaffold scenes—isolating as they do the participants in the act of passion and likewise reflecting the community's knowledge of the crime committed—have long been pointed to as an example of this symbolic design.[8]

Perhaps more than the structural control, however, the dominance of the central symbol is illustrative of the ways in which romance follows its own laws rather than the laws of plausibility. The scarlet letter, the emblem of the act, never leaves center stage from the moment Hawthorne introduces the token to the book's last words—the epitaph found on the tombstone over Hester Prynne's and Arthur Dimmesdale's graves. Indeed, before he first mentions it, Hawthorne foreshadows the red emblem with the wild rose that contrasts so vividly with the dark prison and somber, drably clothed crowd of citizens. In a similar manner, many of the book's images mirror the bright and startling beauty of what Hawthorne labels the ignominious letter on Hester Prynne's breast. Most obvious reflections of the letter are the descriptions of youthful Hester and later of her child.

The initial portrait Hawthorne paints of Hester emerging from her cell clearly equates the two images—Hester with her shining mane of dark hair, rich complexion, and beautiful gown, and the exquisitely embroidered glowing letter. Similarly, Pearl's appearance, with her bright complexion, dark, glowing hair, and rich beauty, is little more than a restatement of Hawthorne's first description of her mother. Further, the child's attire—her crimson tunic embroidered with gold threads—is explicitly compared with the token Hester wore. Yet these reflections of the brilliance of the scarlet letter do not make the images merely emblems of a romantic lack of restraint, thus contrasting the positive passion of Hester and Dimmesdale with the repressive values of the community. Hawthorne is, as I have already observed, working with more than the stark simplicity of allegory. Indeed, the conventional portrait of the lushly beautiful woman with wild, unleashed dark hair is again a description of Hester Prynne; this time she throws off the ignominious letter when she meets Dimmesdale in the forest. By varying the convention, Hawthorne is complicating the symbolic function of the central image. The letter is a sign representing her passion, shame, and repression.

With myriad reflections, Hawthorne creates what John Dolis has termed expressive counterparts. When Hawthorne develops an image, Dolis argues, he "breaks up the object into a momentary mosaic of disparate planes which destroy the organization in depth."[9] By de-emphasizing the realistic dimensions of the object in this way, Dolis continues, Hawthorne focuses the reader's attention on the object's significance. Although Dolis is specifically discussing the fragmenting of one particular image into various aspects, his conclusions are likewise applicable to Hawthorne's technique of creating parallel and contrasting images. The repeated mirror images of the token—the wild rose living in the shadow of the prison, the descriptions of the mother or child, the ache in Dimmesdale's breast, or the strange mysterious light illuminating the sky at Hester and Dimmesdale's midnight meeting at the scaffold—are expressive counterparts showing the rich complexity of the text's central symbol.

Writers of romance may develop or explore their central ideas or problems in many different ways. What characterizes them as romance writers is the way in which their fictional choices de-emphasize the mimetic aspects and instead draw the reader's attention to the surface and abstract dimension of the component as a construct. This abstracting of the work's components focuses on the significance of the image over experience. Examples of this technique may be found in all parts of the work's structure, from its largest formal characteristics to its most delicate stylistic flourishes. The word "ignominious," for example, echoes throughout Hawthorne's tale in Hester's thoughts, Chillingworth's words, and the narrator's descriptions of Hester's predicament and the community's treatment of her. Although Hawthorne repeats the word without variation, having it issue from the different observers allows him to focus on the various perspectives and evaluations of Hester's shame and, consequently, to illuminate his complex view of her public humiliation.

Although *The Scarlet Letter* may seem almost too neat an example of the aesthetic definition of romance, other carefully crafted romances show similar control of the modulation of atmosphere to illuminate and explore an idea. The first book of Spenser's *Faerie Queene*, for example, provides a fairly clear example of the way idea informs a text's fictional components.[10] Spenser's first book illustrates the journey to holiness. Although he uses both political and religious allegory, his choices of illustrations—episode or character, metaphor or image, trope or scheme—show the signs of romance. Rather than relying on simple correspondence of idea and image, Spenser elaborates and embroiders his images, which are informed by the central idea of holiness, to establish the spatial relationships on his canvas. Even the smallest figure may become the expressive counterpart of an idea; for example, Spenser describes the Red Cross Knight's reaction to the lust of the false spright who feigns the shape of Una: "The eye of reason was with rage yblent" (I, ii, 43). The metaphor creates an antithesis so that the key terms are set in balanced opposition—eye and yblent, reason and rage. Perception and the understanding that comes from reason are consumed—indeed physically replaced—by the flames of rage, much as the positive words on the page are contained with the bracket of the destructive words. Because of the figure, the reader sees the destructiveness of ire reflected in one small phrase. Thus, the line reinforces what the reader discovers through following the Red Cross Knight's actions and reactions: ire is a dangerous barrier on the journey toward holiness.

Rhetorical Characters

Much as schemes or tropes, characters in romance can be seen as minor forms, or rhetorical devices, which are both structural and thematic. In a recent study of character in fiction, Baruch Hochman notes that characters in some works simply represent traits or values. Characters in romance, he observes, form part of a pattern—whether psychic or spiritual. They are "an elusive ensemble of psychic qualities that form a composite of something: not necessarily of a person, but of a psychic state and a moral pattern."[11] As with other elements of romance, the character's realistic traits are subordinated to their thematic functions, and consequently such characters do not assume lives of their own. Rather than bringing experiences to the text that allow them to fill in gaps and thus to live with the character, the readers of a romance observe the characters in romance as representatives or expressive counterparts of ideas. The reader may become interested in the characters; however, such interest rarely concerns their personalities in and of themselves, but rather how they embody the formal logic of the text. Although readers are interested in the fate of Spenser's Red Cross Knight, for example, such concern is detached from the sort of identification with him that one would experience with a character in a novel.

Because of this connection to thematic or formal unity, romance characters are frequently experienced, according to Northrop Frye, as features of the mental landscape of the text.[12] In fact, Frye points to differences in characterization as the central issue in distinguishing prose romance from novels. The novelist, he says, "deals with personality, with characters wearing their *personae* or social masks," whereas the romance writer "deals with individuality, with characters in *vacuo* idealized by revery."[13]

The distinction between mimetic characters and complex, individuated, but abstract characters is particularly helpful in identifying and refuting fundamental misconceptions about romance characters. Critics of romance typically assume one of two positions that lead to problematic critical practices. One group, assuming that romance characters are narrowly defined, consequently ignores the techniques the authors use to develop their characters; in other words, these readers overlook what may be seen as the complexity of individuation. The other group, noticing that some romance characters have complexity (that is, they have several different *traits*, the term commonly employed), considers such characters to be functioning mimetically; thus, they are regarded as anomalies—at worst, the author's mistakes and, at best, the author's intuitive recognition that all characters ought to have psychological depth. In both cases, the critics view romance from a mimetic perspective.

The first observation that romance characters are abstractions or conventions does not logically justify the conclusion that writers of romance rarely develop distinct or differentiated characters. Evidence against such a conclusion is found in a second observation. Romance characters frequently can have a complexity that, when viewed as a mimetic dimension, makes them appear to have psychological depth. Indeed, as Edwin Muir observed sixty years ago, conventional characters do not inherently lack complexity simply by representing abstract ideas or ideals. Likewise, it is no more the case that by having complexity, such characters represent possible persons.[14]

Because they are evaluating romance characters with mimetic biases, critics from both groups rarely do justice to the potentialities of romance. Those who believe romance characters have little or no complexity may overlook much of the symbolic resonance, whereas those who see contradictory attributes of characters as a sign of the writer's poor judgment may miss the fullness of the author's design. Although the critics who observe what they call mimetic depth are at least opening discussions of previously neglected characters, their conclusions often imply the kinds of qualitative evaluations associated with the flat/round distinction E. M. Forster suggested. Having observed less than successful realistic characters in a work, these readers may view the works in which such characters are found as primitive and ill formed rather than as fictions with different motives.[15]

The distinction between individuated and mimetic characters may help the reader who observes complexity of character to draw conclusions consonant with theories of romance purpose. That is, a romance character may have various attributes that may make the character appear, in places in the text, to be an individual—without functioning together to create the total portrait of what Seymour Chatman calls the open-ended character, or the kind of character who is capable of changing and thus surprising the reader. In realistic fiction, Chatman argues, the reader senses an agglomeration of traits of a potential person, which can be as enigmatic as those personalities encountered in day-to-day exchanges. Conversely, in antirepresentational fiction the reader views what Chatman has called a teleological set of characteristics.[16] The attributes develop the complexity of the character in all its facets but de-emphasize the realistic quality of the portrayal. Further, because the various aspects of the character cohere (thematically but not psychologically), they present a paradigm that becomes emblematic of idea.

In *Sir Gawain and the Green Knight*, for example, Gawain displays a set of individual traits when he stands before the court and addresses Arthur, asking permission to assume the Green Knight's challenge to exchange a blow for a blow; when he verbally spars with Lady Bertilak in the bedroom scenes in which he attempts to defend himself from her seductive stratagems; and when he hurls the green lace from him after recognizing his guilt in accepting the lady's gift. In each case, his manner of speaking in particular creates the vivid portrait, and, in fact, his responses have a psychological ring of truth. In the first scene, Gawain speaks as the nephew of the king, and, as such, he diplomatically reminds Arthur of his responsibilities to remain at court rather than allowing his excessive pride to tempt him to take on the Green Knight's challenge. To forget his position and its responsibilities, Gawain intimates, would thereby risk not only the reputation of the court but also its safety and stability. In the second series of scenes, Gawain must demonstrate the courtesy of the Arthurian court without yielding to the temptation to be discourteous to his host. In the final scene, the young chastised knight shows his chagrin as he gradually faces and acknowledges his own excessive pride and transgression. He first exhibits mortification, then anger, self-pity, and, finally, humility.

Although the three scenes give Gawain a certain amount of complexity, they do not work together to create a coherent portrait of a possible person. Gawain's responses ring true because of a general and shared psychological truth—he reacts at each point as one would expect a young, courteous, conventional knight placed in such a situation to respond. Nonetheless, the poet shows little interest in developing connections between Gawain's behavior in these three scenes and his behavior elsewhere in order to create a coherent character with psychological depth. Instead, the poet uses just enough individuation as is necessary for the effect produced by these scenes; consequently, he shows Gawain responding in ways appropriate to the combination of the demands of his dominant traits and those of the narrative context. Moreover, in each scene, the psychological situation is subordinate to the controlling idea. Gawain's courtesy and humility in the first scene, for example, are presented in a carefully balanced, rhetorically ornate speech to contrast the king's hasty and brief acceptance of the the knight's challenge. When the Green Knight scoffs at his court, Arthur responds:

> "Sir, now we see you will say but folly,
> Which whoso has sought, it suits that he find.
> No guest here is aghast of your great words.
> Give to me your gisarme, in God's own name,
> And the boon you have begged shall straight be granted."
>
> (323–27)[17]

Observing his uncle's anger and recognizing the danger to the court, Gawain interrupts the impending exchange with:

> "I beseech, before all here,
> That this melee may be mine."
> "Would you grant me the grace," said Gawain to the king,
> "To be gone from this bench and stand by you there,
> If I without discourtesy might quit this board,
> And if my liege lady misliked it not,
> I would come to your counsel before your court noble.
> For I would find it not fit, as in faith it is known,
> When such a boon is begged before all these knights,
> Though you be tempted thereto, to take it on yourself
> While so bold men about upon benches sit,
> That no host under heaven is hardier of will,
> Nor better brothers-in-arms where battle is joined;
> I am the weakest, well I know, and of wit feeblest;
> And the loss of my life would be least of any;
> That I have you for uncle is my only praise;
> My body, but for your blood, is barren of worth;
> And for that this folly befits not a king,
> And 'tis I that have asked it, it ought to be mine,
> And if my claim be not comely let all this court judge,
> in sight."
>
> (340–60)

Seeing these two speeches so closely placed in the text, the reader immediately is struck by the contrast in length, formality, and pace. In addition to demonstrating the proper role of king and courtier, and illustrating the dangers of excessive pride, the words slow down the action. Thus, the reader can assess the situation, along with the court, and acknowledge Gawain as the appropriate character to take on the task and be exemplar of the poet's tale.

Any coherence we perceive as readers is a coherence of idea—the three scenes represent stages in the lesson of the text. Gawain, the reader, and, some might argue, the court learn an important lesson in humility and grace. In romance, then, the elaboration of character development exists in order to develop the poet's particular theme, and with their structural, even abstract, complexity, romance characters are particularly suited to emblematic presentation of the world view of an author.[18]

The Rhetoric of Dialogue

One of the traits characterizing English romances since the earliest translations from their French sources has been the tendency of English romancers to excise passages of soliloquy, or any development of the thoughts and feelings of the characters. These writers craft characters by word and action alone—sometimes more by word than action. Although the thoughts and descriptions of characters are certainly included in many romances written since the Middle Ages, romance characters in subsequent centuries continued to be defined to a great extent by the words they speak.

Consequently, one particularly fertile approach to the study of the rhetorical use of character is through an examination of the style of direct discourse, an approach frequently undertaken in the study of mimetic characters. Certainly, to create rhetorical characters, a romance writer must work with the same narrative techniques as the author of a novel; as Frye has observed, the antirepresentational artist has at his disposal the same materials as the realist. The writer of fiction works within the conventions of language, grammar, and rhetoric. One way these writers use language to craft their texts is by defining their characters by the words they speak.[19] Like the writers of representational fiction, the authors of romances employ language conventions when defining characters through dialogue.

Dialogue may be, in fact, potentially one of the most productive ways the romancer has of elaborating ideas. Because the verisimilitude of mimetic fiction resides extensively in the writer's development of characters, and dialogue is one of the primary means used to illustrate that verisimilitude, readers may see the differences between the two genres most vividly in the words characters speak. Although dialogue in novels seems uniquely appropriate to the speaker, in romances speeches often impress the reader as either appropriate to the narrative situation (if not necessarily to the speaker) or inherently striking. The formal characteristics may be so pronounced and "unnatural" that the reader becomes aware of the images created, and contemplates the words as components in a pattern rather than thoughts of a potential person. Studies of the dialogue of mimetic characters most often concern themselves with the ways that dialogue is used to create lifelike characters.[20] The words a character speaks are considered decorous if they suggest a natural voice or vividly illustrate the idiosyncracies of the character. When it receives attention in studies of romance, dialogue is viewed as interesting only to the extent that it highlights the character traits of a particular type—most often in an exaggerated or hyperbolic manner.

Critics of medieval romance in particular have specifically examined stylistic techniques that romance writers choose to create the character types they portray in their works. Charles Muscatine, for example, in *Chaucer and the French Tradition*, demonstrates the ways form and style distinguish Duke Theseus from the contending lover-knights in "The Knight's Tale" and thus point to meaning. Although the speeches of Palamon and Arcite present questions and suggest human variety and variability, Muscatine argues, those of Theseus progress in a logical and orderly manner and, by doing so, represent the human attempt to maintain social order.[21] Similarly, Cecily Clark, in *"Sir Gawain and the Green Knight:* Characterization by Syntax," argues that the poet differentiates characters by assigning unique speaking styles, and similarities in syntax suggest similarities in type. Clark gives evidence of syntactic similarities to support her argument that Gawain's guide to the Green Chapel is similar in type to the Green Knight/Bertilak.[22] Associating typical speech patterns with classes of characters is also one of the methods that P. J. C. Field identifies in Malory's *Morte Darthur* to characterize the hermits of the "Grail" section of *Le Morte Darthur*, for example, as well as to distinguish knights from other characters.[23] In addition, Ralph W. V. Elliot in *Chaucer's English* discusses the ways Chaucer creates different idiom, or registers, for his various character types.[24] Finally, John Stevens explains the way Gawain's speeches in *Sir Gawain and the Green Knight* identify him as a type of courtesy figure.[25]

None of these stylistic studies of romance, however, explores ways by which romance writers may create complexity in the portrayal of one character, or, similarly, differentiate between characters of the same general type (for example, Palomon from Arcite) in order to explore the complexity of an idea. Presumably, to identify a character as type is to reject any notion of character individuation, and to do so, it seems to me, is to overlook many of the rhetorical possibilities of romance characters. Of the various discussions listed earlier, only Muscatine's, with its consideration of the relationship between character and argument, begins to address the issue.

The potential complexity may be seen by examining a particularly problematical example from Sir Thomas Malory's *Le Morte Darth-*

ur. Having been captured by Sir Mellyagaunt, Guinevere sends a
messenger to Lancelot asking his aid. When Lancelot finally appears
before the queen, she calmly inquires, "Sir Launcelot, why be ye
so amoved?"[26] Viewing this question as one spoken by an "open-
ended" character, one would have to suspect some underlying
meaning beneath the surface of the queen's words—perhaps a certain coquettishness as she toys with her paramour. In fact, at least
one critic has viewed Guinevere's dialogue as displaying the complexity of a psychologically developed character, her words reson-
ating, meaning more than she says or perhaps conveying subtle
messages to her listener.[27] Although this is an attractive theory in
many ways, it simply does not go far in explaining Malory's *Le
Morte Darthur*.

To assume that Guinevere is a complex character whose words
illustrate psychological depth is to disregard her many shifts in role
and concurrently in voice. If, instead, one tries to account for the
speech as words spoken by a romance character, the question
changes. No longer does one wonder what the queen means but
rather how the words work rhetorically within the larger framework
of *Le Morte Darthur*. Because speech is no longer seen as part of a
larger mimetic portrayal of Guinevere—but rather as words that
develop dimensions of her character—determined by character
type, narrative context, or controlling idea, one must look at the
surface structure and the pattern it presents.

Among the possible explanations, three come to mind immediately and seem more plausible than the mimetic view. First, in her role
as noble queen, Guinevere often represents a kind of stability within
the court, particularly in the early books. For example, she frequently acts as an arbiter of justice, judging the knightliness of chivalric acts. The speech might be seen then as a reminder to the
reader of her role as queen. In additon, Guinevere always speaks
formally when she addresses Lancelot in the presence of others, and
thus one might conclude that narrative context demands particular
speech conventions of a queen. The third explanation, however,
complicates the interpretation and shows the way the interplay of
demands of character type, narrative context, and controlling idea
can create thematic complexity in romance. This scene immediately
precedes a change in Lancelot's behavior—for the first time, he defends Guinevere's innocence on a technicality when Mellyagaunt
accuses her of sleeping with one of her men and thus committing
treason against the king. Her words illustrate perhaps too sudden a
shift in context, a non sequitur, even a coquettishness (if one sees
coquettishness to be a rhetorical rather than a mimetic trait), but the
focus is on the context rather than the personality of the queen. The

change may then exemplify or predict a change in the portrait of Lancelot as ideal knight and indeed in the stability in the fellowship itself.

In addition to creating complexity through shifts in tone and context, the romance writer may use dialogue to develop and explore an idea through subtle formal and stylistic markers. This textual surface may reveal more than the explicit meaning necessary to any particular situation. Rather, it may point to large issues in the work. When, for example, late in *The Scarlet Letter*, Pearl comments on her observation that the sunshine avoids her mother, her periods are brief and intensified as exclamations, thus creating a rapid pace:

> "Mother," said little Pearl, "the sunshine does not love you. It runs away and hides itself, because it is afraid of something on your bosom. Now, see! There it is, playing, a good way off. Stand you here, and let me run and catch it. I am but a child. It will not flee from me; for I wear nothing on my bosom yet!"[28]

Pearl's words are of less interest to the reader as a part of some psychological profile of the young child than they are as signs of Hester's mood. The rapidity contrasts the flickering sunlight and its expressive counterpart in movements of the child with the somber, resolved woman. At the same time, Pearl's words prefigure her own movement into the sunlit excitement of hope and cheerfulness. Likewise, they introduce a scene that will be as intense and brilliant, yet brief and flickering as the sunlight and the words themselves. This bit of speech has implications beyond the particular situation as it calls to mind the larger structural movement of the tale. The language itself, then, can be seen as an expressive counterpart, helping to reveal the world view of the romancer. In reading the dialogue associated with a romance character, we look beyond the character to the significance of the construct.

Instead of merely examining ways in which speeches serve to establish character types, as most critics of romance have, we may approach such dialogue by putting aside the dominant assumptions and exploring the hypothesis that romance characters can be and often are complex. They may even sometimes have what I will call individuation; when they do, the tension between the individuation and type creates the thematic, or rhetorical, function of the character. The task of critics when they encounter conventional characters is to examine the ways the writer subtly uses literary devices to create the kind of intricate texture that embodies the idea behind the textual canvas.

2
Queenly Decorum in *Le Morte Darthur*

The characters in *Le Morte Darthur* are recognizable by *genus*—knights exhibit varying degrees of knightliness, queens queenliness, and so forth. Indeed, they display all of the characteristics Edwin Muir long ago pointed to as the criteria for typed characters.[1] In the first place, they respond with typical and appropriate rather than idiosyncratic behavior. In addition, they are never given the opportunity to express their private thoughts; indeed, as Mark Lambert has observed, *Le Morte Darthur* is "strikingly apsychological."[2] Finally, Malory's characters have the sort of complexity Muir attributes to typed characters—a complexity not less true but merely different from that of round characters. Such complexity, Muir explains, is created when characters are expressed by more than one formula. In *Le Morte*, characters gain complexity by playing several different roles.

In a recent discussion of Malory's titles, Dhira Mahoney discusses the ways Malory enhances the complexity of his narrative by applying formulaic labels. Mahoney contends that Malory sees his characters "in terms of the roles they are filling at the time,"[3] and argues that he indicates a character's role change by assigning different appropriate titles to the same person in different roles. She shows, for example, that Malory distinguishes between Isode's roles as King Mark's queen and as Tristram's lover by calling her "quene Isode" in the first context and "La Beale Isode" in the second. Such epithetization shows different facets of Isode's character but does not suggest that she differs from other characters who play similar roles. In a manner parallel to his use of epithets, Malory also creates such complexity, it seems to me, by choice of speech conventions in dialogue.

Malory's tendency to substitute dialogue for narrative has long been recognized as one of his dominant stylistic characteristics. Although many readers of *Le Morte Darthur* describe this dialogue as lively and vivid, they also insist on its lack of individuality.[4] The apparent contradiction in the two observations is acknowledged by at least one critic who attributes the liveliness of Malory's speeches to their brevity and performative function, and maintains that they remain characteristic of type rather than individual: "Malory is wonderfully good," Mark Lambert argues, "at making his dialogue both normative and vivid."[5]

In a recent challenge to this standard position, Peter R. Schroeder attempts to show that in one particular case Malory has created a character with psychological depth. Examining the speeches of Guinevere in *Le Morte Darthur*, Schroeder observes variety and incongruity, which lead him to conclude that she is "plausible, individual, and inconsistent in the way 'real people' often are." Thus, he argues, "Her speech, concealing as much as it reveals, keeps hinting at something inarticulate but psychologically 'real' beneath its surface."[6]

As radically different as these two positions appear, ultimately the findings, if not the conclusions, may be reconcilable. In fact, a third possibility exists. Although Malory's characters are conventional, they are also complex in ways that stretch the traditional notions of typed characters. Schroeder is absolutely correct in his observation that Guinevere's speeches exhibit apparent non sequiturs. Yet, admitting an element of individuality does not warrant finding *Le Morte Darthur*'s dialogue psychologically revealing. It is rather metaphoric, and thus his characters finally are emblems that represent Malory's vision of the human condition.

In *Medieval Romance: Themes and Approaches*, John E. Stevens defines medieval romance characters as types with their individual traits developed in order to represent ideals.[7] Discussing Chaucer's Troilus, for example, Stevens contends that Chaucer is more interested in the general or ideal than in the particular or individual; thus, Stevens sees Troilus as a representative of an ideal. Further, Stevens finds unidealized characters foils for the idealized. "One should assume," he argues, "all modifications of this ideal world to be attempts to make it more meaningful and to communicate it more forcefully."[8] A reader can find contrast similar to the one Stevens sees between characters in the portrayal of individual characters. Malory often makes one character represent several different types to create not psychological depth, as Peter Schroeder argues, but rather a detailed and complex representation of human nature. A comparison of the speeches of Guinevere and Isode will illustrate this technique.

The story of Tristram and Isode in many ways mirrors that of Lancelot and Guinevere. Indeed, the two tales provide parallel motifs: both Guinevere and Isode are queens whose paramours are the most noble knights of their respective courts. In addition, their stories have several parallel episodes: both are captured by knights; both remain at court while the knights pursue adventures; both are separated from their lovers during a time when the knights, in madness and exile, wander the forest. Whatever Malory's ultimate purpose in narrating two tales of love triangles, the similarities and contrasts between the stories offer a special opportunity to examine Malory's techniques of characterization by means of discourse.

As the same societal type, the two queens speak in remarkably similar styles. They differ very little in mean sentence length, number of sentences per speech, number of words per speech, and number of clauses per sentence.[9] Their average numbers of main clauses, dependent clauses, and phrases are practically the same. They also have similar percentages of grammatical elements. Adjectives, nouns, and verbs, for example, vary less than one percentage point.[10] Their sentence openings display a basic similarity as well. Both characters rely most heavily on five sentence openings: coordinate conjunctions, subjects, vocatives, interjections, or adverbial disjuncts used as interjections (e.g., certainly, truly), and verbs. Of these openings, both most often use the coordinate conjunction or the vocative.[11]

In addition to this syntactic resemblance, each queen frequently echoes the other by uttering the same formula or parallel syntactic structure in similar narrative contexts. Several examples show these stylistic similarities. First, when questioned by their kings about suits brought against them, each queen responds simply with the same formula. Following Sir Mador's demand that he be allowed to avenge the murder of his cousin, Arthur asks Guinevere for her explanation of the poisoned apple. She responds simply, "Sir as Jesu be me helpe!" (1051). In a similar context, Palomydes demands that Isode abide by her promise to accompany him from Mark's court. When Mark turns to his queen for an explanation, she responds, "Hit is as he seyth, so God be me helpe!" (421). In two later episodes, each queen requests information about the other. Guinevere asks: "How doth sir Trystram . . . and La Beall Isode?" (764), and Isode asks: "How faryth my lorde Arthure, and quene Gwenyver, and the noble knyght sir Launcelot?" (616). Finally, their syntax shows remarkable similarities when, fearing for the lives of their lovers, they express their sorrow. Guinevere tells Lancelot, "I woll [nat] lyve long aftir thy dayes" (1166), and Isode prays, "I may nat lyve aftir the deth of sir Trystram de Lyones" (499).

Not only do the speeches of the two queens show general stylistic resemblances, they also follow a similar pattern of modification according to context.[12] Both queens speak in four principle contexts: they converse with kings, captors, knights, and their lovers. Each context elicits a particular style. Addressing their kings, both queens speak far more formally than in any other context, displaying the brevity and understatement, which P. J. C. Field associates with the noble syntax of a knight. Such a style, Field notes, expresses "a certain self-restraint and fortitude."[13] Each speech addressed to a king is short, its clauses linked by coordinate conjunctions, its nouns unmodified. For example, when Guinevere reponds to Arthur's directive to accompany him to battle, she replies, "Sir . . . I am at youre commaudement, and shall be redy at all tymes" (127). Similarly, Isode replies to greetings from Arthur with, "Sir . . . ye ar wellcom" (743), and later with, "Sir, God thank you! . . . Of youre goodness and of youre larges ye ar pyerles" (757).

Guinevere and Isode also exhibit stylistic similarities when speaking to the errant knights who capture them. Both address their captors somewhat more tersely than when they address other knights. Captured by the knight who would be her paramour, Isode tells him, "wete thou well, I feare nat gretely to go with the, howbeit thou haste me at avauntage uppon my promise. For I doute nat I shall be worshypfully rescowed fro the" (421). Likewise, Guinevere, attacked by Mellyagaunt, advises him:

> Traytoure knyght . . . what caste thou to do? Wolt thou shame thyselff? Bethynke the how thou arte a kyngis sonne and a knyght of the Table Round, and thou thus to be aboute to dishonore the noble kyng that made the knyght! Thou shamyst all knyghthood and thyselffe and me. And I lat the wyte thou shalt never shame me, for I had levir kut myne owne throte in twayne rather than thou shoulde dishonoure me! (1122)

These examples and other speeches when they address their captors are marked by an absence of adjectival modification as well as by frequent object clauses, imperatives, and second-person pronouns—both use the familiar *thou* to remind their captors of their difference in rank. In addition, both characters shift from the formal to informal second-person pronoun to contrast respect and distance with intimacy, contempt, or difference in rank. In Isode's capture scene, she first addresses Palomydes with the formal and polite *ye* before she discovers how he intends to have her repay her debt to him: "Sir, I shall abyde you," she says respectfully, "I wote nat wat is your desyre, but I woll that ye were, howbeit that I profyrde you largely, I thought none evyll, nother, I warne you, none wyll I do" (420). Once he reveals his demand, however, she subtly reminds him of the difference in their social positions by addressing him with the familiar thou. Guinevere, conversely, first addresses Mellygaunt with the contemptuous thou when she admonishes him for his crime. When he kneels before her to beg her mercy, however, she no longer needs to remind him of her authority and consequently resumes her formal role: "'What ayles you now?' seyde quene Gwenyver. 'Parde, I myght well wete that some good knyght wolde revenge me, thoughe my lorde knynge Arthure knew nat of thys your worke'" (1128).

Despite their similarities, the two speeches differ and, as such, indicate a distinction Malory is drawing between the two situations and thus show the interaction of the demands of role and context. Isode's speech exhibits the restraint of ceremonial speeches addressed to a noble man, with its balance of short clauses and phrases, absence of adjectives, and modification through simple adverbs or adverbial phrases. In contrast, although Guinevere's speech is formal, it illustrates a quite different emotional context. It has a two-part crescendo, each section building to an admonishment—for bringing dishonor to the king, in the first section, and to the queen, in the second. The speech begins with two short questions, then continues with rather dense parallelism as Guinevere enumerates Mellyagaunt's crimes. The series of clauses build the intensity to the extended verbal phrase "to be aboute to dishonore" and the protracted object "the noble kynge that made the knyght." It is as though the piling up of clauses, phrases, and modifiers becomes emblematic of the ramifications of Mellyagaunt's attack. The subsequent sentence then returns to the shorter period, its less complex structure stressing the significance of the knight's act. The three-part structure repeats the syntax of the previous sentence but in simpler form, reinforcing and thereby making perfectly clear the insult to the king and the fellowship. Finally, in the last sentence, the shame and dishonor are joined in parallel clauses, and the vivid "I had levir kut myne own throte in twayne" illustrates the intensity of her response.

The verbs in the two passages are dissimilar as well. Although Isode's verbs are restrained (wete, feare not, haste, doute not, and shall be rescowed), Guinevere's are charged, and the language intensifies the importance of her predicament and its potential effect on the entire fellowship. She contrasts her determination not to be dishonored (clearly expressed in the verbal levir kut) with Mellygaunt's decision (implied in the verb caste) to capture her and thus dishonor himself, her, and the fellowship, whereas the refrain of shame, dishonoure, shamyst, shame, dishonoure is a constant reminder of the disgrace he is bringing to them all.

These differences demonstrate the contrast in the two narrative contexts. Guinevere's capture, unlike Isode's, is an insult to the fel-

lowship of the Round Table as well as to its king. As such, Mellygaunt violates not merely a general knightly code but the particular
knightly code he had vowed to uphold as a knight of the Round
Table. By capturing the wife of the king who pronounced the code,
Mellygaunt violates the code, and, in addition, offends both Guinevere and the fellowship of the Round Table both explicitly and symbolically. Further, the capture of Guinevere in many ways marks
one stage in a sequence of events leading to the breakdown in the
unity of Arthur's court. As a result of these events, Lancelot will be
captured and separated from the fellowship, and, with his other ab-
sences, his capture demonstrates the gradual disintegration of the
once-unified and strong society of knights.

Sir Palomydes' capture of Isode, conversely, carries none of this
complex resonance. First, Mark's court is never portrayed as a noble fellowship. Further, although Palomydes is a knight, he is not a
member of Mark's court. Nor does the capture of Isode in actuality
violate a code. Palomydes' demand that Isode grant his wish was
justified by the vow Isode made and would not break. Thus,
although parallel, the two capture episodes differ. Guinevere's
anger and disdain are not only justifiable but necessary given the
nature of her capture. The capture of Isode, however, although
perhaps reprehensible, does not warrant such contempt; this difference in the demands of narrative context is reflected when contrasting particular styles. Despite these differences, however, the
speeches generally exhibit similarities, particularly when compared
with the characters' manners of speaking in other contexts.

Addressing knights other than captors, the two queens speak with
somewhat longer sentences, with greater modification, as well as a
concentration of nouns. Two examples show the resemblance in
style. Guinevere sends Pediver on a pilgrimage to Rome:

> But this shall I gyff you in penaunce: make ye as good skyffte as ye can,
> ye shall bere this lady with you on horsebak unto the Pope of Rome, and
> of hym resseyve youre penaunce for your foule dedis. And ye shall nevir
> reste one nyght thereas ye do another, and ye go to ony bedde the dede
> body shall lye with you. (286)

In a speech that in many ways echoes Guinevere's Isode watches the
battle of Palomydes and Tristram. After seeing Palomydes weaken-
ing, she stops the fight and banishes him:

> This shall be thy charge: thou shalt go oute of this contry whyle I am
> [therin]. . . . Than take thy way, . . . unto the courte of kynge Arthure,

and there tell her that I sende her worde that there be within this londe but four lovers, and that is sir Launcelot and dame Gwenyver, and sir Trystrames and quene Isode. (425)

Both speeches show the dominant characteristics of dialogue with knights—both exhibit far greater complexity of syntax than speeches addressed to kings or to their captors. In addition, the two speeches are remarkably similar in form. Both begin with clauses containing the demonstrative "this" referring forward to adjunctive clauses, the nominal clause combining simple imperative and imperative with temporal auxiliary: in Isode's speech, "thou shalt go," "take," and "tell," in Guinevere's speech, "make," "ye shall bere," "ye shall nevir reste," and "resseyve." Further, both speeches extend the adjunctive clause by means of sequential coordinate clauses and, in addition, include prepositional phrases of direction: "unto the Pope of Rome" and "unto the courte of Kinge Arthur." Finally, the two speeches rely heavily on short clauses and a high frequency of nouns.

Although the characteristic styles of the two queens remain similar in speeches addressed to kings, captors, and knights, they are distinctly differentiated in the fourth context. A most remarkable contrast can be seen in their conversations with their paramours; this pattern of differentiation is ultimately emblematic of the human condition. Although both queens vary their style when speaking to their lovers, they change in rather different ways. The contrast can be seen both in their private and public conversations.

Isode's two most intimate conversations with Tristram occur within the seclusion of Joyous Guard, Lancelot's abode, where Isode and Tristram take refuge after fleeing Mark's court. In both cases she speaks more like a chiding wife than a lover, and in both cases she advises Tristram through innuendo rather than direct statements. Each speech has a parallel in a speech of Guinevere's in a similar narrative context. In the first set of parallel episodes, each queen expresses concern for the safety of her lover and, consequently, advises him to act with caution. Isode says:

I marvayle me muche that ye remembir nat youreselff how ye be here in a straunge contry, and here be many perelous knyghts, and well ye wote that kynge Marke is full of treson. And that ye woll ryde thus to chace and to hunte unarmed, ye myght be sone destroyed. (683)

In contrast, Guinevere gives Lancelot advice in a direct and forceful manner:

I warne you that ye ryde no more in no justis nor turnementis but that youre kynnesmen may know you, and at thys justis that shall be ye shall have of me a slyeve of golde. And I pray you for my sake to force yourselff there, that men may speke you worshyp. But I charge you, as ye woll have my love, that ye warne your knyyesmen that ye woll beare that day the slyve of golde uppon your helmet. (1103)

In the second set of parallel episodes, both Guinevere and Isode give their lovers advice on appropriate decorum. In parallel episodes, Lancelot and Tristram wish to withdraw from knightly functions rather than attend without their lovers. Isode responds:

God deffende . . . for than shall I be spokyn of shame among all queyns and ladyes of astate; for ye that ar called one of the nobelyste knyghtys of the worlde and a knyght of the Rounde Table, how may ye be myssed at the feste? For what shall be sayde of you amonge all knyghts? 'A! se how sir Trystram huntyth and hawkyth and cowryth within a castell wyth hys lady, and forsakyth us. Alas!' shall some sey, 'hyt ys pyte that ever he shuld have the love of a lady.' Also, what shall queyns and ladyes say of me? 'Hyt ys pyte that I have my lyff, that I wolde holde so noble a knyght as ye ar from hys worshyp.' (839–40)

And in the speech echoing the form of Isode's earlier speech, Guinevere says:

Sir, ye are gretly to blame thus to holde you behynde my lorde. What woll youre enemys and myne sey and deme? 'Se how sir Launcelot holdith hym ever behynde the kynge and so the quene doth also, for that they wolde have their plesure togydirs.' (1065–66)

Despite the similarity in the form and subject, the variations in the style of these speeches reflect the difference in the two queens' roles as lovers. Although Isode is defined throughout *Le Morte Darthur* in terms of her relationship with Tristram, her speeches never display the intimacy of Guinevere's private speeches to Lancelot. Although Guinevere's speeches display density and economy, Isode's have a chatty, informal quality exhibited by looseness and verbosity. For example, Guinevere speaks in parallel clauses with ellipsis when she warns Lancelot that their enemies will judge their actions: "sir Launcelot holdith hym ever behynde the kynge, and so the quene doth also." She continues with an adverbial clause of purpose, "for that they wolde have thier plesure togydirs," which unites the two clauses and the two lovers in the repeated third-person personal pronoun they and the intensive adverb togydirs. Similarly, in her speech giving Lancelot her sleeve, she begins the three sentences of advice with three parallel commands: she "warns," "prays," and "charges" him.

Isode also uses words and clauses parallel in content and grammatical function but without the tightness and balance of Guinevere's. Anticipating the inevitable gossip of the court concerning Tristram's breach in decorum, Isode warns him in three loosely parallel clauses that some knights and ladies will gossip: "A! se how sir Tristram huntyth and hawkyth and cowryth"; "Alas! . . . hit is pite that ever he was knyght"; and "hyt is pyte that I have my lyff." This loose parallelism is also seen in her earlier advice that Tristram not ride unarmed when she warns him with three clauses parallel in function but not in syntax. She observes in amazement that "ye remembir nat yourselff how"; "well ye wote that"; and "ye will ryde thus." The loose parallelism continues in the two clauses that are the objects of "ye remember nat": "how ye be in a straunge contry" and "here be many perelous knyghts." In each case, despite their parallel functions in the sentence, the clauses are not parallel in structure and thus lack the density exhibited by Guinevere's parallelism.

In addition, Isode's speeches display a repetitiveness that contrasts with the economy of Guinevere's speeches. Although Isode uses three quotations to illustrate the shameful gossip, in the parallel speech, Guinevere uses only one. In addition, Isode's amplification intensifies rather than extends; as she lists his attributes, she multiplies Tristram's guilt but does not explain his offense. She calls Tristram one of the noblest knights of the world and a knight of the Round Table. Isode, however, describes his unknightly activities as, first, hunting and hawking, and, second, cowering within a castle with his lady and forsaking his companions. The amplification illustrates his guilt but does not necessarily make the reader (or Sir Tristram) understand the knight's offense. Likewise, in the earlier speech, Isode warns Tristram of the danger of his environment with three clauses: he is in a strange country, the country is filled with dangerous knights, and King Mark is full of treason. Again, the extensions add no new information but rather emphasize her argument.

The style of Isode's conversations with Tristram also differs in the level of formality from that of Guinevere's intimate conversations with Lancelot. Although Guinevere's private speeches to Lancelot display a looser and longer period than her public speeches, they do not approach the informality of Isode's. In fact, Malory seems to distinguish between informality and intimacy, and one way he does so is in the use of pronouns. Unlike Guinevere, Isode never addresses Tristram with the familiar thou in her role as lover. Thus, although she may speak informally, she does not speak intimately. Guinevere, conversely, addresses Lancelot with the formal ye in public, but with the intimate form in some private conversations. She shifts to the familiar thou in four separate episodes, and, in each episode, Malory underlines the familiar form by repeating it throughout the speech. Twice, she addresses her lover with the contemptuous thou, first when she discovers Lancelot in Elaine's bed and exclaims:

> A, thou false traytoure knyght! Loke thou never abyde in my courte, and lyghtly that thou voyde my chambir! And nat so hardy, thou false traytoure knyght, that evermore thou com in my syght! (805)

In the second episode she questions his fidelity and cries out with anguish and contempt:

> Sir Launcelot, now I well understonde that thou arte a false, recrayed knyght and comon lechourere, and lovyste and holdiste otheir ladyes, and of me thou haste dysdayne and scorne. For wyte thou well, now I undirstonde thy falsehede I shall never love the more, and loke thou be never so hardy to com in my syght. And ryght here I dyscharge the thys courte, that thou never com within hit, and I forfende the my felyship, and uppon payne of thy hede that thou se me nevermore! (1047)

The other two instances show affection rather than contempt. In the first, Lancelot prepares to leave Guinevere to fight his accusers when Aggravayne and Mordred discover the lovers in the queen's chamber. Before taking his leave, Lancelot renews his vows of love and assures Guinevere that if he is killed, his kin will rescue and protect her; Guinevere responds, "Nay, sir Launcelot, nay!. . .Wyte thou well that I woll <nat> lyve longe aftir thy dayes" (1166).[14] Similarly, in her final farewell, Guinevere repeatedly addresses Lancelot with the intimate thou as she vows never again to see him and implores him to depart from her. Gradually, however, she shifts from the personal to the formal form and thus marks her attempt to end the relationship both in fact and in spirit, the polite ye helping to distance her from her lover. Her first speech includes frequent repetition of thou: "I requyre the and beseche the hartily, for all the lo[v]e that ever was betwyxt us, that thou never se me no more" (1252). By the end of this speech, she begins to shift to the polite form: "[Go] to thy realme, [an]d take ye a wyff." In her second speech, she has changed almost entirely to the polite form with only one instance of the intimate: "A, sir Launcelot, if ye woll do so and holde thy promyse! But I may never beleve you . . . but that ye woll turne to the world agayne" (1253). By her third and final speech, she has abandoned the use of thou entirely: "Nay, . . . that shal I never do, but absteyne you from suche werkes" (1253).

Isode addresses Tristram with thou in only one episode—when she bids farewell at his departure from Ireland. Realizing that she will probably never see him again, she reponds to his departing: "A jantyll knyght! . . . full wo I am of thy departynge, for I saw never man that ever I ought so good wyll to" (392). In this episode, Malory uses Isode's shift from the intimate to the polite form to indicate a change in their relationship. Like Guinevere's change in the pronoun in her final farewell to Lancelot, Isode's shift to the polite form indicates a distancing of the characters. Isode addresses Tristram intimately *before* he has identified himself as the son of a king; after his revelation, however, she shifts immediately to the polite ye and never again addresses him with the intimate thou.

In addition to the second-person, the first- and third-person plural pronouns define the differences between the two queens in their roles as lovers. Although Isode never refers to herself and Tristram jointly by the first- or third-person plural pronoun, Guinevere uses the form in three episodes. As in the use of the familiar singular form, Malory emphasizes the plural form by repetition. In the first episode, quoted earlier, Guinevere advises Lancelot of his knightly duty; she first refers to "their" pleasure, then intensifies the closeness of their relationship with the adverb togydirs. In the second episode, when Guinevere and Lancelot are discovered together in the queen's chamber, she uses both the nominative form and the possessive: "Now ar we myscheved bothe!" and "I dred me sore oure longe love ys com to a myschyvus ende" (1165). Finally, in the last episode, the pathos resonates through the plural pronouns: "Thorow oure love that we have loved togydir is my moste noble lorde slayne" and "all the lo[v]e that ever was betwyxt us" (1252). In this final parting from Lancelot, the repetition of the first-person plural pronoun becomes a refrain, a poignant reminder of their love and a recognition of the tragic consequences of that love: "Thorow oure love that we have loved togyder is my moste noble lorde slayne . . . for all the love that ever was betwyst us that thou never se me no more . . . thorow the and me ys the fl[ou]re of kyngis and [knyghtes] destroyed" (1252).

The two queens' manners of addressing their lovers also demonstrates the difference in relationships. Guinevere generally addresses Lancelot with sir or sir Lancelot, but with the contemptuous vocative, "thou false traytoure knyght," when she discovers him in

Elaine's bed. Guinevere's shift to the contemptuous address both emphasizes the intensity of her anger and marks the beginning of her jealousy and doubt of Lancelot's loyalty. It is also at this point that she banishes Lancelot from the court, an action that results in his descent into madness. In the parallel episode between Tristram and Isode, the scene leading to the madness and exile of Tristram, Isode is the accused party. Thus, Isode has no reason to address Tristram with the contemptuous form, and indeed she does not.

In other narrative contexts, as I have indicated, Guinevere maintains the conventional, ceremonial vocative when addressing Lancelot—thus giving a dignity and formality to their relationship absent from the relationship of Tristram and Isode. In contrast, Isode frequently addresses Tristram with my lorde, particularly when she is fearful. In the first episode when she uses the alternate form, Isode fears Tristram will slay Palomydes before the Saracen might be christened; in the second episode, she fears that King Mark will banish or kill Tristram; and in the third, she is fearful that Tristram will be killed in a tournament. Even when fearful, however, Guinevere maintains the ceremonial vocative. She speaks to Lancelot only once in fear, when Aggravayne and Mordred discover the lovers in the queen's chamber. Because Lancelot has no arms or weapons with which to defend himself, Guinevere fears he will be slain and she burned. Yet she gains control over her fear. She vows that if he is slain, she will accept her death as meekly as ever did any martyr, and she wishes to sacrifice her life so he might escape. Resolutely, controlling her fear, she addresses Lancelot with the formal and dignified sir Launcelot.

Not only are the two queens dissimilar in parallel episodes in their roles as lovers, they differ in an even more fundamental way, and the contrast illustrates their different functions in *Le Morte Darthur*. Isode's discourse style remains constant whether she speaks to Tristram in public or private. Guinevere's style, in contrast, changes remarkably. Although she maintains formal decorum in public conversations, in private, she expresses her emotional attachment to Lancelot and, indeed, displays a range of emotions. By contrasting the two styles, Malory makes the private relationship an important issue in *Le Morte Darthur*. Their illicit love is different from the acceptable relationship illustrated in their formal and public behavior.

In contrast, Malory makes no distinction between the public and private relationship between Tristram and Isode. Throughout *Le Morte Darthur*, Isode is defined precisely in terms of her rela-

tionship with Tristram. All of her speeches are either directed to
Tristram, concerned with her relationship with him, or spoken in
conjunction with or at his side, or with the assumption that her lover
will soon be with her. Despite the greater emphasis on Isode's role
as paramour, however, there is little variation in their relationship
whether they are seen in public or private situations. In addition,
Isode's style of discourse when addressing Tristram remains constant regardless of the context. Although Isode is technically Tristram's queen by virtue of her marriage to King Mark, she never
speaks to him in the ceremonial voice as Guinevere addresses Lancelot in similar situations. Likewise, she never speaks to him in
the intimacy of her chamber. In fact, the conversations between
Tristram and Isode generally occur in a semiprivate or public context, and these speeches vary little in length or level of formality.
For example, in the presence of knights at a tournament, Isode expresses her concern for Tristram's safety:

> Myne owne lord. . . for Goddys sake, be ye nat displeased wyth me, for
> I may none othirwyse do. I saw thys day how ye were betrayed and
> nyghe brought unto youre dethe. Truly, sir, I sawe every dele, how and
> in what wyse. And therefore, sir, how sholde I suffir in youre presence
> suche a felonne and traytoure as ys sir Palomydes? For I saw hym wyth
> myne yen, how he behylde you whan ye wente oute of the fylde. For
> ever he hoved stylle uppon his horse tyll that he saw you com agayne-
> warde; and than furthwythall I saw hym ryde to the hurte knyght, and
> chaunged hys harneys with hym, and than streyte I sawe hym how he
> sought you all the fylde, and anone as he had founde you he encountred
> wyth you, and wylfully sir Palomydes ded batayle wyth you. And as for
> hym, sir, [I] was nat gretly aferde, but I drad sore sir Lancelot whyche
> knew nat you." (755–56)

In a semiprivate parting (with only Dame Brangwayne in atten-
dance), she exclaims:

> A, my lorde, sir Tristram! Blessed be God ye have youre lyff! And now I
> am sure ye shall be discoverde by this lityll brachet, for she woll never
> leve you. And also I am sure, as sone as my lorde kynge Marke do know
> you he woll banysh you oute of the contrey of Cornwayle, othir ellis he
> woll destroy you. And therefore, for Goddys sake, myne owne lorde,
> granunte kynge Marke hys wyll, and than draw you unto the courte off
> kynge Arthure, for there ar ye beloved. And ever whan I may I shall
> sende unto you, and whan ye lyste ye may com unto me, and at all tymes
> early and late I woll be at youre commaundement, to lyve as poore a lyff
> as ever ded quyene or lady. (502)

The two speeches exhibit many similarities. Both begin with the vocative my lord rather than the more formal sir or sir Tristram; in fact, the public speech begins with what seems to be a more personal "myne owne lord" whereas the private parting begins with the addition of the more formal title and name. In addition, in both speeches the sentences are extended by hypotaxis, and the clauses in each joined loosely by coordinate conjunction, often with adverbs or adverbial phrases: "and then," "and now," "and ever whan," "and therefore," or simply "for," and both speeches rely heavily on adverbs or adverbial phrases for modification. The few adjectives are, in the main, past participles: displeased, betrayed, hurte, brought, discoverde. Each speech contains much repetition as well. In the public, "I saw" is repeated five times, then the variant "he behylde" and "he saw"; in the private, "I am sure" occurs twice, "he woll" twice, and "I may" and then "ye may." Although both speeches express Isode's attachment, they pale when set by expressions of Guinevere's passion for Lancelot in lines such as, "A sir Launcelot, Launcelot! Ye have betrayde me and put me to the deth, for to leve thus my lorde!" (872).

The dialogue between Lancelot and Guinevere occurs in contexts from the very formal on of the court to the very intimate, private one of the bed chamber, and Guinevere's style of speaking changes according to these different contexts. In the presence of other knights at a tournament, for example, Guinevere formally addresses Lancelot with "Sir, I requyre you that any ye juste ony more, that ye juste wyth none of the blood of my lorde kynge Arthur" (661), and after the same tournament with "Sir, well have ye done this day!" (662). In a private parting, however, she addresses him intimately: "Alas. . . that ever I syghe you! But He that suffered dethe uppon the Crosse for all menkynde, He be unto you good conduyte and saufte, and all the hole felyshyp!" (872). As these representative examples show, the syntax of her public speeches to Lancelot is tighter and more balanced than that of her private ones. The public speeches contain short clauses with little modification, whereas the private speech's interjection and subsequent nominal clause suggest the informality of conversational speech—modifiers not only lengthen the sentences and thereby loosen the structure but also indicate her emotional state. In addition to the stylistic contrast between public and private speeches, Guinevere's style also differs among her private speeches, in which she expresses a range of emotions including anger, sorrow, exasperation, fear, and remorse. In each case, the style changes.

This disparity between public and private styles accounts for some puzzling passages in *Le Morte*. In "The Fair Maid of Astolat" episode, for example, Guinevere formally reprimands Lancelot for his treatment of Elaine: "Sir . . . ye myght have shewed hir some bownte and jantilnes whych myght have preserved hir lyff" (1097). This scene occurs shortly after Guinevere refuses to receive Lancelot, because he has worn the Maid's colors in the tournament at Winchester.[15] Were Guinevere a consistent, idiosyncratic character, the first passage would be puzzling, its tone perhaps ironic. Because Guinevere's discursive style depends on conventions of context, however, and because she addresses him publicly in this scene, the speech is appropriate.

Guinevere's variety in style in her role as lover becomes clear when compared with Isode's relative stability, and, further, with Guinevere's own consistency in other roles. Her stylistic inconsistencies suggest a certain ambiguity or even divisiveness in her character. In other words, the pattern of her speeches expresses her condition of being divided against herself, and thus discourse becomes representative of character. Given this apparent individualization of Guinevere, we might argue, with Peter Schroeder, that she is something of an anomaly in the Middle Ages, a character with the psychological depth usually associated with characters in the novel. Such a view would certainly explain evaluations such as Charles Moorman's when he argues that she is truly an unattractive character who become more and more quarrelsome, jealous, and nagging throughout the later books.[16] Although she certainly is an unattractive character in most of the seventh tale and the beginning of the eighth, her character has more facets than such an evaluation as Moorman's would indicate. In fact, she is consistently noble in the early books, remains a noble figure in the middle books, and finally becomes, in the end, almost saintlike. Before abandoning the dominant critical position, then, we ought to attempt an explanation that accounts for Guinevere's multifaceted character within the definition of typed characters.

The essential question must be not whether a character possesses several different traits—or even whether those traits are contradictory—but whether the paradigm, as Seymour Chatman puts it, is teleological and thus indicative of flat character or agglomerate and indicative of a round one.[17] Certainly, Schroeder would argue the second. Another view is possible. The dialogue of Malory's parallel queens illustrates the distinction between the traditional notion of typed character and individuation within the bounds of character type.

Such a distinction is similar to the medieval romancer's use of narrative form, a distinction Larry Benson has discussed in his study of *Le Morte*. Benson explains that the narrative organization of English romance relies on a thematic pattern, or what Northrop Frye calls the mythic structure, but also exhibits a realistic element on the episodic level. For example, Benson calls the early Middle English *King Horn* a "realistic" work because "many of its episodes have the sort of cause-and-effect motivation that we expect in 'realistic' works." Nonetheless, although episodes may appear realistic, Benson finds the overall structure to be controlled by theme rather than motivated by some sort of causal consistency. Causality within episodes then exists to develop the idea of the poem rather than to create a linear, coherent plot. The same structural principle, Benson argues, operates in Malory's *Le Morte Darthur*, and because modern readers are accustomed to reading realistic, horizontal narratives, when they encounter horizontal episodes, they assume Malory is trying to write modern, well-plotted narratives rather than creating a montage of episodes that function together to present a thematic pattern.[18]

The thematic principle applies to Malory's notion of character as well, and serves well to explain why Malory's characters can be at once type and individual. It is certainly true that, as P. J. C. Field has observed, all knights exhibit the same speech characteristics[19] as long as we add "except when they don't" because it is equally true that at times they seem to speak, as Mark Lambert has indicated, vividly and with directness and vigor.[20] In fact, Malory does differentiate similar types but does so by distinguishing between the roles they play. Two characters who represent the same type will display the same manner of speaking in similar contexts but will exhibit apparently individual characteristics in different contexts that demand different conventions; thus, the dialogue has the appearance of plausible speech. Because the role the character plays determines the contexts, however, the characterization is thematic or determined by a controlling principle.

To determine Malory's purpose in individuating Guinevere, we must begin then by asking how Malory's characters represent his particular vision of truth. An answer lies in the queen's relationship to the Round Table and the sentiment expressed by the code of the Table. Guinevere not only is the wife of the king who establishes and keeps the code but also brings the Round Table to Arthur's court as part of her dowry. Further, her wedding to Arthur provides the occasion for establishing the fellowship and its code of behavior. She is first the respectful wife of the king. Not merely a figurehead, she even accompanies her king and his retinue to battle during the war with the five kings. She shows her nobility in this episode in both words and deeds, responding to her king with a quiet dignity and the tone of a respectful subject. When Arthur directs her to prepare to accompany him to battle, Guinevere readily obeys: "Sir. . .I am at youre commaundement, and shall be redy at all tymes" (127). When, in the heat of battle, Arthur subsequently allows her to decide whether to attempt the treacherous crossing of the Humber or to remain and face the battle, she chooses the action appropriate for a queen and responds: "Yet were me lever to dey in ths watir than to falle in your enemyes handis. . .and there to be slayne" (128).

In addition, she is the gracious hostess of the court. She greets visiting knights and ladies, presides over tournaments, and commends knights on their prowess. As in her replies to Arthur, her ceremonial speeches as hostess are marked by an appropriate formality, or what Mark Lambert has called "the coldness which is the special mark of her royalty."[21] The sentence are balanced, relying on coordination rather than subordination, and polysyndetic in their abundance of coordinate conjunctions. The diction is direct, simple, and unadorned. She uses few adverbs and no adjectives. Speaking in her role as hostess, she grants Morgan Le Fay leave to remain in the country or to leave when she desires "You may abyde. . .tyll youre brother the kynge com home. . . .Well. . .ye may depart whan ye woll" (150). As the king's representative at the tournament at Surluse, she demands of Lancelot: "Sir, I requyre you that and ye juste ony more, that ye juste wyth none of the blood of my lorde kynge Arthur" (661). And at the same tournament, she commends Sir Lamerok on his valor: "Sir, well have ye done this day" (662).

Finally, she acts, in the early tales at least, as a kind of judge of knightly behavior. Three particular instances show her speaking in this capacity. In the first, she pronounces blameworthy the unknightly behavior of King Pellinor; in the second, she praises Sir Kay's valor in the war with the five kings; in the third, she finds King Pediver guilty of the murder of his wife. Eugène Vinaver notes that none of the pronouncements are found in Malory's French source (1333, 1340, 1426). In the second episode, Guinevere's speech was one of Arthur's remarks in the source. In the third instance, the entire episode apparently is original. These changes are particularly noteworthy because the speeches in the three episodes function together to identify Guinevere with the knightly code.[22]

In order to underscore the tragic fall of the once-exemplary fellowship, Malory contrasts the later instability of the knights with their essential nobility in the first few books. Likewise, Guinevere's behavior in the early books is virtuous and her language illustrates her nobililty. In "The Book of Sir Tristram," however, Malory begins to develop her relationship with Lancelot, and thus creates a tension between Guinevere in her noble role as Arthur's queen and her role as Lancelot's paramour. At this point in the tale, Malory seems to leave the state of the relationship between Lancelot and Guinevere ambiguous for two reasons. In the first place, his references to their adultery are explicit in the later books, as is his description of the Tristram-Isode relationship from its inception. Second, and perhaps more convincing, no evidence of Guinevere's private style of speaking appears until the "Lancelot and Elaine" episode toward the end of "The Book of Sir Tristram." Instead of an explicit relationship, then, forebodings occur throughout "The Book of Sir Tristram" of the treasonous relationship: Lancelot accompanies Guinevere to the tournament at Surluse; he tells her that he is harboring Tristram and Isode at Joyous Guard; he repeatedly refers to her beauty; and Tristram and Isode, whose story parallels that of Lancelot and Guinevere, fall in love and then live openly in adultery.

Despite the forebodings throughout "The Book of Sir Tristram," Guinevere, like the chivalric society, remains essentially noble, and thus her response to Lancelot's infidelity in the "Lancelot and Elaine" episode is startling. Full of wrath, she rebukes Lancelot and calls him a false knight; yet after hearing his explanation, she immediately relents. Eugène Vinaver notes that Guinevere's forgiveness of Lancelot is not found in Malory's source and seems inconsistent with his account of subsequent events.[23] This explanation, however, seems to be precisely the point of the addition; Guinevere's response is altogether improbable and out of character. In fact, from this episode until her final farewell to Lancelot, Guinevere's behavior and style of speaking vacillate from noble, ceremonial, and public to passionate, varied in emotion, and private.

Guinevere's final scene, however, shows her altering her behavior to return to her proper ceremonial and thus noble role. Rather than maintaining the setting in the privacy of the queen's chamber, as found in the stanzaic *Morte Arthur*, Malory places the lovers in a cloister with the queen attended by her ladies. The more formal setting allows her to begin by addressing the ladies who attend her with a formal, unadorned speech: "'Ye mervayle, fayre ladyes, why I make thys fare.' 'Truly, . . . she seyde, . . . hit ys for the syght of yondir knyght that yondir stondith. Wherefore I pray you calle hym hyddir to me'" (1252.3–.5). When she turns to speak to Lancelot, however, she shifts to the style and tone characteristic of her private conversations with her lover. The sentences lengthen immediately; the syntax becomes more complex, with extensive embedding. Her use of first-person plural and second-person singular pronouns also marks the intimacy of the speech: "Thorow thys same man and me hath all thys warre be wrought, and the deth of the moste nobelest knyghtes of the worlde; for thorow oure love that we have loved togydir is my moste noble lorde slayne. Therefore, sir Launcelot, wyte thou well I am sette in suche a plyght to gete my soule [hele]" (1252.8–.13).

The change in style adds a poignant note but also reminds the reader of the public consequences of their private sin. Gradually, as Guinevere recalls the magnitude of their sin, she discards the intimate style of speaking found in her private conversations with Lancelot for the polite style of her formal speeches and thus attempts to distance him from her. After repeating, in condensed form, her opening confession of responsibility for the downfall of the fellowship, she begins the process of becoming more formal: "And therefore [go] thou to thy realme, [an]d there take ye a wyff, and lyff with [hir wyth] joy and blys" (1252.26–.27). Her syntax once again becomes simpler and paratactic, the period shorter with little modification, and the polite form of the second-person pronoun begins to appear. In her second speech, her sentences are even shorter, and she has shifted to the polite form of the pronoun with only one exception: "'A, sir Launcelot, if ye woll do so and holde thy promyse! But I may never beleve you,' seyde the quene, 'but that ye woll turne to the worlde agayne'" (1253.7–.9). By her third and final speech, her words are brief and she has abandoed thou entirely, shifting irrevocably to the formal ye: "'Nay,' sayd the quene, 'that shal I never do, but absteyne you from suche werkes'" (1253.27–.28). The change in style marks her attempt to end the adulterous relationship both in fact and in spirit. Although she is for a time divided against herself and inconstant in her fluctuations in emotions, Guinevere ends speaking once again like a queen. Thus, the paradigm of her discourse, which reflects the development of the fellowship of the Round Table, expresses a positive view of the chivalric society. It may be inevitable that men and women fail to live up to society's ideals, but the quest, Malory shows us, is a glorious one, and those who attempt it are finally noble.

3

Platonic Ideas in the *New Arcadia*

The *New Arcadia* has long been recognized as the work of a consummate stylist.[1] Certainly few, if any, critics of Sir Philip Sidney's prose would deny his skill as a craftsman. What historically has been at issue, however, is whether Sidney's superbly crafted style represents merely his concern for ornament or functions, rather, as an important determiner of the meaning of the text. Recent studies of the *New Arcadia* have maintained the second. Arthur Amos, for example, has argued that "Sidney's prose tends to be analytic in a way that reveals the complexity of problems,"[2] and Thelma Greenfield has been somewhat more direct: "word by word and phrase by phrase," she says, the *New Arcadia* "does encapsulate extended meanings in the smallest units."[3] Among other observations of the way style functions as a determiner of textual meaning, both Amos and Greenfield note the way dialogue reveals the nature or mind of the speaker. Given the *New Arcadia's* many speeches with their marvelously complex rhetorical flourish, the next step in the criticism of the *New Arcadia* would be to examine the relationship between Sidney's dialogic style and his notion of character.

In *Idea and Act in Elizabethan Fiction*, Walter R. Davis identifies the use of romance characters as one of the defining features of early fiction, concerned as it is with human relationship to the ordered world. Romance characters differ from characters in novels, Davis explains, because whereas the novel "explores the general through particular aspects of human life," the romance "faces generic concerns—problems of good and evil, of man in the universe—in a direct, almost abstract way."[4] Davis does not discuss the role dialogue plays in developing romance characters, but an extension of his analysis of Sidney's poetic theory may address the question. Davis observes that Sidney, like other Renaissance thinkers, was interested in the relationship between an Aristotelian definition of poetry as an art of imitation and a Platonic view—or "going beyond Nature to Ideas for imitation."[5] In fact, a study of the speeches in the *New Arcadia* shows Sidney developing characters who represent ideas, or ideals, as well as actors in a story, thus contributing to a fiction that aptly illustrates Sidney's poetic theory, a fiction Davis describes as follows:

> Such fiction will remain as close to ideas, ideals, or ideas as to actions; and it will thus, instead of rendering for us the probabilities of life as we know it, attempt to enlarge our sense of the possibilities of life. It will dwell in the various areas of contact between things as they are and things as they might be, and it will end by presenting to our minds some potential adjustment between the two.[6]

Norman Friedman's *Form and Meaning in Fiction* contains a useful scheme for an examination of such romance characters. He delineates three types of attributes, or traits, that characters exhibit to varying degrees. These traits he identifies as individual, general, and universal. He argues further that although characters may possess a combination of these attributes, the particular form of the work determines the proportion. Friedman contends that characters in mimetic works exhibit predominantly individual traits, whereas those in didactic works exhibit predominantly general or universal traits. Applying Friedman's character-trait distinctions to characters of a didactic romance such as Sidney's, we might posit two catagories of character types: the societal and the philosophical. Representatives of the first category are dominated by general traits (those shared "with other members of his class, his culture, his time, and his histroy") and the second by universal ones (those shared "with all of mankind, regardless of time and place"). The latter, Friedman argues, are "elemental, basic, fundamental, mythic, permeating."[7]

Sidney's characters in the *New Arcadia*, like Malory's, represent types who are defined by their positions within their social order. The Arcadian world is inhabited by princes, princesses, kings, queens, shepherds, and shepherdesses, who either behave appropriately to their stations or, like Basilius, are noteworthy for their inappropriate behavior. Indeed, Sidney's exemplary characters teach social responsibility through the method he outlined in his *Defense of Poesie*: "as the image of each action stirrith and instructeth the mind, so the loftie Image of such woorthies, most enflameth the mind with desire to bee woorthie: and enformes with counsaile how to be woorthie."[8]

In addition to providing lessons in social manners and responsibilities, Sidney's characters exemplify philosophical ideals, although the author might not make a distinction between the social and philosophical so clear. These complex character types both enflame the mind with desire to be worthy and provide models of ways in which one might be worthy. Such an approach, Fulke Greville described as: "to limm out such exact pictures, of every posture of the mind, that any man being forced, in the straines of life, to pass through any straights, or latitudes of good, or ill fortune, might (as in a glass) see how to set a good countenance upon all the discountenances of adversitie and stay upon exorbinant smilings of change."[9]

Certainly, Sidney develops societal types as exemplary characters to teach the responsibilities accompanying social status. When two characters are of the same type, they possess the same attributes, traits that represent the class, culture, time, and history. Yet, in addition to providing lessons in social manners, Sidney's characters exemplify philosophical ideals and thus display attributes that are elemental, basic, fundamental, mythic, and permeating rather than representative of social position. Nancy Lindheim has commented on this multidimensional quality of Sidney's characters, noting that characters of the same type share the same attributes, and yet, she observes, one can see shades of emphasis that "are actually predispositions for one sort of behavior or experience rather than some other."[10] In fact, a study of dialogic style shows that the interplay of the manners of societal rank, philosophical characteristics, and the demands of the plot results in multidimensional characters. Two characters, for example, may represent the same societal type yet play different roles and, in addition, represent different philosophical types. We can observe this complexity by examining the dialogue of one of Sidney's many pairs of parallel characters, whom Lindheim has called the most important example of Sidney's tendency to present character by means of antithesis: the two princesses, "Pamela and Philoclea."

A brief outline of the plot demonstrates the ways in which Sidney marks their resemblances. The two princesses are daughters of King Basilius of Arcadia, who has retired with his family into pastoral seclusion where he keeps his daughters isolated from men. Two princes, the cousins Pyrocles and Musidorus, are shipwrecked on the coast of Laconia and separately make their way to Arcadia and eventually to Basilius's retreat, where they fall in love with the two princesses. Each prince disguises himself with the intention of wooing one of the sisters. During the princes' sojourn in the forest, wild beasts pursue the princesses. Pyrocles, in his disguise as Zelmane the Amazon, slays a lion and rescues Philoclea; Musidorus, disguised as Dorus the shepherd, kills a she-bear to rescue Pamela. Later, the two couples engage in tale telling, and gradually the princes win the hearts of the two princesses. The two sisters, along with Zelmane, are captured by their Aunt Cecropia, who attempts to persuade one of the sisters to wed her son. Both decline and are tortured by their aunt. Although Sidney does not complete his revision, we might assume that he would have followed the general outline of the original *Arcadia,* and that we would find the two princesses wed to their suitors and reconciled with their father.

Because Philoclea and Pamela are both princesses who illustrate the appropriate manners of ladies of nobility, their speech patterns bear a number of shared characteristics. In formal speech, for example, both use rather long sentences. These lengthy sentences are expanded by means of extensive embedding, suspending, and interrupting with clauses and verbal phrases. Two sentences show the princesses' formal speaking style. In the first, Pamela suspends the main clause to the very last moment, following a series of introductory dependent clauses:

> And as absurd it is to thinke that if it had a beginning, his beginning was derived from Chance: for Chance could never make all thinges of nothing; and if there were substances before, which by chaunce shoulde meete to make up this worke, thereon followes another bottomlesse pitte of absurdities.[12]

Similarly, Philoclea suspends the main clause of her sentence by means of series of dependent verbal phrases:

> For, having in vaine attempted the fardest of her wicked eloquence, to make eyther of us yield to her sonne, and seeing that neither it, accompanied with great flatteries, and riche presents, could get any grounde of us, nor yet the violent way she fell into cruel lie, tormenting our bodies, could prevayle with us; at last, she made either of us thinke the other dead. . . . (488)

Despite this tendency toward the long, hypotactic sentence, both princesses often use the tight economy and density of antithesis and paradox, employing parallel structure and, frequently, ellipsis. Pamela addresses her God as the life of all "to whom nothing is either so great, that it may resist; or so small, that it is contemned" (382). Later, she implores Musidorus, with ellipsis, "Let my name live in thy mouth, in thy harte my memory" (473). Likewise, Philoclea responds to Amphialus's advances with antithesis: "you call for pittie, and use crueltie; you say you love me, and yet do the effectes of enmitie" (368). Later, in disguise, she advises Zelmane not to mourn the apparent death of her lover, playfully using paradox and ellipsis: "See the folly of your passion (said she) as though you should be neerer to her, you being dead, and she alive; then she being dead, and you alive: and if she be dead, was she not borne to die?" (486).

The formality of this noble style becomes more striking when compared to the style characteristic of other societal types. First, the speeches of Pamela and Philoclea are distinctly different from those of the rustics, Miso and Mopsa. A comparison of the four women's tales of Cupid reveal the differences. The tales begin:

> Miso: I was a young girle of a seven and twenty yeare old, and I could not go thorow the streate of our village, but I might heare the young men talke: O the pretie little eies of Miso; O the fine thin lips of Miso; O the goodly fat hands of Miso: besides how well a certaine wrying I had of my necke, became me. (238)

> Mopsa: In time past (sayd she) there was a King, the mightiest man in all his country, that had by his wife, the fairest daughter that ever did eate pappe. Now this King did keepe a great house, that every body might come and take their meat freely. (241)

> Philoclea: Of late there raigned a King in Lycia, who had for the blessing of his mariage, this onely daughter of his, Erona; a Princesse worthie for her beautie, as much praise, as beautie may be praise-worthy. (232)

> Pamela: The father of this Prince Plangus as yet lives, and is King of Iberia: a man (if the judgement of Plangus may be accepted) of no wicked nature, nor willingly doing evill, without himselfe mistake the evill, seeing it disguised under some forme of goodnesse. (242)

The most obvious distinction between the two types is in the level of diction. Miso and Mopsa rely on concrete nouns, such as streate, village, eies, man, and house, and commonplace, even homely, expressions, such as "a certain wrying I had of my necke" and "that ever did eate pappe." In contrast, the speeches of Philoclea and Pamela contain many abstract nouns, such as blessing, beauty, judgement, and nature, and more formal expressions, such as "for the blessing of his marriage" and "if the judgement of Plangus may be accepted." Their metaphors are also quite different. Although Miso and Mopsa use rather obvious similes such as "like a hangman upon a pair of gallowes" (238) and "as dark as pitch" (241), the princesses describe with metaphor or example. Philoclea describes Erona's love for Antiphilus, for example, as a knot that "might well be cut, but untied it could not be" (235), and Pamela shows her contempt for the King of Iberia by describing his wooing with a metaphor of a fisherman: "And she . . . lefte no arte unused, which might keepe the line from breaking, whereat the fishe was alredy taken; not drawing him violently, but letting him play himself upon the hooke, which he had greedely swalowed" (244).

In addition to the contrast in diction, syntax also shows the differences between societal types. The sentences of the two rustics tend to be paratactic. When they do include subordinate construction, they add modification after main clauses, such as in Miso's speech:

This monster sat like a hangman upon a paire of gallowes, in his right hand he was painted holding a crowne of Laurell, in his left hand a purse of mony, and out of his mouth honge a lace of two faire pictures, of a man and a woman, and such a countenance he shewed, as if he would perswade folks by those alurements to come thither and be hanged. (238)

In contrast, the two princesses' sentences are hypotactic, dense with their extensive embedding, such as in Pamela's speech:

Whereupon, the King (to give his fault the greater blow) used such meanes, by disguising himselfe, that he found them (her husband being absent) in her house together: which he did, to make him the more feelingly ashamed of it. (243)

Finally, the styles differ beyond the syntactic level. Miso and Mopsa narrate loosely connected tales, Mopsa repeatedly introducing sentences with "and so," Miso with "then" or with no clear transition. In contrast, Pamela and Philoclea note the development of their narratives with clear transitions, as in Philoclea's "but before she could accomplish all the solemnities" (233) or Pamela's "and because he might bende him from that" (243). Thus, their tales evolve gradually, with each sentence carefully linked to the previous one.

In addition to differing from the style of the two rustics, the two princesses' noble manner of speaking differs also from that of their father, who is a representative of nobility in conflict with itself. Although the differences are subtler, they are nonetheless distinct. Like the sentences of the two princesses, those of Basilius are highly hypotactic; however, Pamela and Philoclea maintain tight logic—their interruptions have specific purposes—whereas Basilius frequently goes beyond the judicious use of amplification. When Philoclea tells Zelmane of Cecropia's attempt to coerce one of the sisters into marriage with her son, the princess's numerous modifying phrases and clauses amplify without adding superfluous detail:

> And when I (for thy sake especially deare Pyrocles) could by no force, nor feare be won, they assayed the like with my sister, by bringing me downe under the scaffolde, and (making me thrust my head up through a hole they had made therin) they did put about my poore necke a dishe of gold, whereout they had beaten the bottome, so as having set bloud in it, you sawe how I played the parte of death (God knowes even willing to have done it in earnest) and so had they set me, that I reached but on tiptoes to the grounde, so as scarcely I could breathe, much less speake. (488)

Basilus's words sound much different from his daughter's when he continues the tale of Plangus and Erona. He begins by modifying with abandon:

> But then to leave that unrepeated, which I finde my daughters have told you, I may please you to understand, since it pleaseth you to demaund, that Antiphilus being crowned, and so left by the famous Princes Musidorus and Pyrocles (led thence by the challenge of Anaxius, who is now in these provinces of Greece, making a dishonorable enquirie after that excellent prince Pyrocles alreadie perished) Antiphilus (I say) being crowned, and delivered from the presence of those two. (330)

Further, although all three characters rely heavily on parallelism, Pamela and Philoclea use many different types in rather more subtle ways than their father does. Often, Basilius is unnecessarily repetitive; in the passage just cited, for example, "It may please you to understand since it pleaseth you to demaund" and "Antiphilus being crowned. . . Antiphilus (I say) being crowned." At other times, he speaks in tight, precise parallel structure such as in "and seeing to like; and liking to love; and loving straight to feel" (333), and "but her witte endeared by her youth, her affliction by her birth, and her sadnesses by her beautie" (333). In these last two examples, the style emphasizes the parallelism: in the first, the blending of anadiplosis and polyptoton stresses the repeated participle plus infinitive structure; in the second, the ellipsis of the participle in the second and third phrases and the repetition of the second-person possessive pronoun and preposition "by" draw attention to the precisely parallel structure.

Unlike their father's, the parallelism of the two princesses is somewhat more delicate, its structure less displayed, even when the components are grammatically parallel. For example, when Philoc-

lea says "so evill could she conceale her fire, and so wilfully perse-
vered she in it" (232), the shift from the past tense verb plus the
modal "could" to simple past tense and, in addition, from simple
object to adverbial phrase distracts the reader from the underlying
parallelism. Even when the components are more precisely parallel,
such as in Pamela's "never suffering his fear to fall nor his hope to
hasten" (244), the structure may seem less overt. In this example,
the alliteration within each phrase draws attention to the similarities
within the phrases and thus, at least momentarily, away from the
repetition in form. Further, they often contain devices such as anti-
metabole as, for example, when Philoclea inverts the order of the
repeated words in "A princesse worthie for her beautie, as much
praise, as beautie may be praiseworthy" (232), or ellipsis as when
Pamela omits the adjective in "whether his wit were greater in win-
ning their favours, or his courage in employing their favours" (264).

Finally, Pamela and Philoclea generally employ metaphor or
figurative language (and these sparingly), whereas Basilius fills
his tale with a variety of comparisons from the simple example,
"like one carried up to so hie a place" (330), to the complex but
homely "like a bladder, sweld redie to breake, while it was full of
the winde of prosperitie" (334), to the paradoxical "as in a picture
which receives greater life by the darkenesse of shadowes, then by
more glittering colours" (333), to the metaphor of a kingdom as a
tennis court "where his subjects should be the balles" (330).

Thus, by contrasting the dialogic styles of the two sisters in their
roles as princesses with other societal types, Sidney develops their
exemplary behavior as representatives of a noble class. In addition
to being types of princesses and thus speaking in an appropriately
noble style, however, Philoclea and Pamela also represent contrasting philosophical types. The first mention of the princesses is, in
fact, a description noting their differences. After Musidorus is res-
cued from the sea, he is taken to the home of Kalander where he
sees a portrait of Philoclea and her parents. Musidorus asks about
the lady, and Kalander tells the story of Basilius and his family and
describes the two daughters:

> The elder is named Pamela; by many men not deemed inferiour to her
> sister: for my part, when I marked them both, me thought there was (if
> at least such perfections may receyve the worde of more) more sweet-
> nesse in Philoclea, but more majestie in Pamela: mee thought love
> plaide in Philocleas eyes, and threatned in Pamelas: me thought Philoc-
> leas beautie onely perswaded, but so perswaded as all harts must yeeld:
> Pamelas beautie used violence, and such violence as no hart could resist:

and it seemes that such proportion is betweene their mindes; Philoclea so bashfull as though her excellencies had stolne into her before shee was aware: so humble, that she will put all pride out of countenance: in summe, such proceeding as will stirre hope, but teach hope good manners. Pamela of high thoughts, who avoides not pride with out knowing her excellencies, but by making that one of her excellencies to be voide of pride; her mothers wisdome, greatnesse, nobilitie, but (if I can ghesse aright) knit with a more constant temper. (20)

From the outset, Pamela represents the philosophical idea of Majesty, and Philoclea symbolizes Beauty, or what Lindheim calls Humility.[13] Sidney contrasts the two by yoking them as parallel yet complementary opposites throughout the text. In one episode, fearing Anaxius's threat to cut off their heads and send them to their father, Pamela and Philoclea await his arrival: "Pamela nobly, Philoclea sweetly" (504). Sidney explicitly notes the contrast again when they comfort each other in the scene before Amphialus comes to them to excuse his role in their imprisonment: "Philoclea tempered Pamelas just disdaine, and Pamela ennobled Philocleas sweete humblenesse" (491). The two princesses are also differentiated by narrative context. Parallel episodes frequently illustrate their differences. Both reside in pastoral seclusion, but Philoclea is in the care of her parents whereas Pamela lives in the home of a local rustic. Both are courted by suitors who disguise their true identities; however, although Pyrocles disguises himself as an Amazon, Musidorus becomes a shepherd. Further, despite the similarities in their stories, both Pamela and Philoclea are at times placed in episodes that have no parallel in the story of the other. Pamela teaches Musidorus the manners of love when he feigns love for the rustic Mopsa. Philoclea laments her love for a woman. Pamela majestically defends her faith against Cecropia's insidious attack. Philoclea mourns with great dignity the apparent death of her sister.

One way Sidney delineates subtle differences between the sisters as philosophical types is by assigning each a unique style of speaking with contrasting diction, syntax, and form when he wishes to emphasize their philosophical virtues. For Beauty, Sidney develops a gentle and courteous, frequently hesitant sytle, for Majesty, an emphatic, self-confident style. In similar contexts, for instance, Philoclea uses simple, unadorned style and Pamela a highly ornamented style; likewise, Philoclea uses passive voice and subjunctives, whereas her sister uses active voice and imperatives. Further, Philoclea always maintains the formality of the second-person pronoun you (except when intimately addressing Pyrocles), whereas Pamela shifts to a contemptuous thee to show disdain. Sidney marks the differences between the philosophical types in parallel and contrasting narrative contexts. Three pairs of parallel speeches illustrate the differentiation within similar contexts.

Both Musidorus and Pyrocles, swept away by affection for Pamela and Philoclea, respectively, attempt a kiss. The princesses' responses are markedly different, the contrast expressed in their manners of speaking as well as in the content of their speeches. Without rejecting Pyrocles' advances, Philoclea gently asks that he allow her to speak. She addresses him with a request in the form of a rhetorical question: "How will you have your discourse (said she) without you let my lips alone?" (308). In contrast to this sweetness, Pamela responds to Musidorus with a wrathful series of imperatives, surely earning Sidney's description of her as a lady possessing just disdain:

> Away (said she) unworthy man to love, or to be loved. Assure thy selfe, I hate my selfe for being so deceived; judge then what I doo thee, for deceiving me. Let me see no more, the only fall of my judgement, and staine of my conscience. (355)

In the second example, Cecropia approaches each princess with her son's offer of marriage. Each episode begins with Cecropia complimenting the princess on her beauty. Again the replies of the two princesses illustrate their essential differences. Philoclea's words are marked by economy, brevity, and simplicity: "Alas Madame (answered Philoclea) I know not whether my teares become mine eyes, but I am sure mine eies thus beteared, become my fortune" (377). In contrast, Pamela replies to Cecropia's compliment with highly ornamented prose. Amplifying through interruptions of qualification, modification, and comparison, Pamela refutes her aunt's definition of beauty and in doing so diffuses her compliment:

> Truely (saide Pamela) I never thought till nowe, that this outward glasse, intitled Beautie, which it pleaseth you to lay to my (as I thinke) unguiltie charge, was but a pleasaunt mixture of naturall colours, delightfull to the eye, as musicke is to the eare, without any further consequence: since it is a thing, which not onely beastes have; but even stones and trees many of them doo greatly excell in it. (403)

Following their discussions of beauty, Cecropia proposes marriage in her son's name. Each princess rejects the offer, and both present their replies with balanced form, beginning by acknowledging the courtesy of the offer but ending by rejecting it. Despite the similarity in the structure of the speeches, however, the two replies differ syntactically. The difference between the two can be seen most obviously in their choice of verbal phrases. Although Philoclea tempers her certain rejection with a courteous subjunctive, Pamela puts off her aunt's offer emphatically with modal auxiliaries and adverbs:

> Philoclea: Aunt (said she) I would I could be so much a mistres of my owne mind, as to yeeld to my cousins vertuous request: for so I construe it. But my hart is already set (and staying a while on that word, she brought foorth afterwards) to lead a virgins life to my death: for such a vow I have in my selfe devoutly made. (379)

> Pamela: Ther is no effect of his love (answered Pamela) better pleaseth me than that: but as I have often answered you, so, resolutely I say unto you, that he must get my parents consent, and then he shall know further of my mind; for, without that, I know I should offend God. (405)

Finally, Sidney contrasts the two princesses according to philosophical types by placing parallel speeches side by side in the same episode; knowing that Anaxius means to avenge the wounding of Amphialus by their deaths, Pamela and Philoclea await his coming and discuss their fate. Again the two speeches differ both in style and content. Pamela speaks first:

> Sister (said she) you see how many acts our Tragedy hath: Fortune is not yet a wearie of vexing us: but what? A shippe is not counted strong for byding one storme? It is but the same trumpet of death, which now perhaps gives the last sounde: and let us make that profite of our former miseries, that in them we learned to dye willingly. Truely said Philoclea, deare sister, I was so beaten with the evils of life, that though I had not vertue enough to despise the sweetnesse of it, yet my weaknesse bredde that strength, to be wearie of the paines of it: onely I must confesse, that little hope, which by these late accidents was awaked in me, was at the first angrie withall. But even in the darkenesses of that horrour, I see a light of comfort appeare; and how can I treade amisse, that see Pamelas steppes? I would onely (O that my wish might take place) that my schoole-Mistres might live, to see me say my lesson truely. (503–4)

Pamela's words show her responding to impending death with a stoical acceptance and noble courage. The speech begins with a series of three clauses that define her philosophical position. The three statements emphasize Pamela's essential wisdom with their implied maxims: Fortune vexes mankind; in order to be strong, a ship must bide many storms; and the trumpet of death will give the last sound. Further, she speaks slowly and deliberately with short clauses and few transitions. This precise delineation of syntactic un-its isolates each statement of understanding. Finally, she demons-trates the nobility of her attitude in her diction: her use of concrete nouns associated with the active, noble life such as ship, storm, and trumpet joined with active-voice verbs suggest her courage.

Philoclea's speech, in contrast, shows an ambivalent response to the threat of death. She finds comfort in the virtuous strength of her sister but feels despair in the prospect or losing the joys of life. Her style demonstrates this dual response in structure, syntax, and diction. The structure of the speech is defined by a contrast of anti-thetical abstract nouns—evil/virtue, sweetness/weakness, darkness of horror/light of comfort—and by paradox: "I had not vertue enough to despise the sweetness of it" and "my weaknesse bredde that strength, to be wearie of the paines of it." Although she accepts her fate, she does not embrace it. Instead, her acceptance is tentative. The speech proceeds haltingly, the long period interrupted fre-quently by clause and phrase. Further, in contrast to the active verbs and imperatives of Pamela's speech, Philoclea's speech relies heavi-ly on passive voice and the subjunctive. Unable to achieve philo-sophical objectivity, Philoclea faces death in the only way she understands—with an emotional response, which she illustrates with her repetition of the first-person pronoun and abstract nouns of sensation.

Although Pamela's strength gives Philoclea courage, Philoclea's poignant remorse softens Pamela's stoicism. Thus, after Philoclea's speech, Pamela speaks a second time, and now her philosophical objectivity is tempered. She gradually shifts to a personal response when she regrets causing pain to her shepherd Musidorus. Sidney signals the change in her attitude by gradually modifying her style of speaking. Her sentences lengthen, she inserts transitions, and, final-ly, her last sentence mirrors Philoclea's hypotactic period:

Were that a life, my Philocolea? said Pamela. No, no, (said she) let it come, and put on his worst face: for at the worst it is but a bug-beare. Joy is it to me to see you so well resolved; and since the world will not have us, let is lose us. Onely (with that she stayed a little, and sighed) onely my Philoclea, (then she bowed downe, and whispered in her eare) onely Musidorus, my shepheard, comes betweene me and death, and makes me thinke I shall not dye, because I know he would not I should dye. (504)

In addition to differentiating the princesses as philosophical types within parallel narrative contexts, Sidney often portrays them in contrasting contexts, which magnify the attributes of their types. He sets Pamela in several episodes demonstrating the just disdain characteristic of Majesty. When Musidorus attempts to steal a kiss, for example, Pamela illustrates angry virtue by rising to the occasion with majestic indignation (quoted earlier). It is Arthur Amos's position that Pamela's response with the intimate thee form of the personal pronoun is ambivalent in tone.[14] This shift in pronoun, however, linked with the directness of her reply precisely demonstrates her unequivocal reaction and makes her statement such an appropriate example of angry virtue. In fact, she uses the informal thee in only eight instances in the text, and in only two of these does she suggest intimacy with its use. Both instances occur in the privacy of soliloquy. In one instance she addresses her God in prayer, and in the other, anticipating her own death, she directs a brief apostrophe to Musidorus. The remaining uses all clearly indicate anger or disdain.

Thus, it seems to me, Pamela's diction in no way suggests ambivalence. Indeed, the decorum of the circumstances requires her indignant reaction. Musidorus violates the boundaries of their relationship and does so in an abrupt, sudden, and violent manner. Pamela's speech demonstrates her control rather than confusion in anger; she banishes and admonishes him with four short clauses marked by their economy. Each clause begins with an imperative, the first and last ending with vocatives of insult: "unworthy man to love, or to be loved" and "the only fall of my judgment, and stain of my conscience" (355). The central clauses conclude with nominal clauses as direct objects, each with prepositional phrases functioning as adverbs. The tightness of the structure surely shows her control and thus indicates not confusion or ambivalence but pride and disdain.

In addition to her angry response to Musidorus, four other situations illustrate Pamela's angry virtue: she refutes Cecropia's attack on faith, scorns her aunt's cruelty, rejects Amphialus's apology, and refuses Anaxius's offer of marriage. Although different in length and content, the speeches have certain characteristics in common. In each speech, she addresses the object of her anger with a disdainful vocative and the contemptuous thee. She addresses Cecropia as "beastly woman," "wicked woman," "foolish woman," and "most wicked woman." Amphialus, she addresses as "traitor" and Anaxius as "proud beast." Further, each speech has at its heart a command and as such relies on the imperative. When Cecropia blasphemously attacks Pamela's faith, for example, the princess interrupts her: "Peace (wicked woman) peace, unworthy to breathe, that doest not acknowledge the breath-giver; most unworthy to have a tongue, which speakest against him, through whom thou speakest: keepe your affection to your self, which like a bemired dog, would defile with fauning" (407).

Having established parallel structure in the exordium, Pamela continues by relying on parallelism to form the framework of her speech and to mark the movement of her argument. Her argument in the first section is structured by the formula "you say X" followed by a refutation of the statement. Gradually, however, she abandons this formula, first modifying it to "but you will say," then "but you may perhaps affirm," and finally to a new formula "if you mean." The final section of the speech builds with a magnificent crescendo of parallel conditional clauses followed by causal clauses to its inevitable conclusion: "that the time will come, when thou shalt knowe that power by feeling it, when thou shalt see his wisdome in the manifesting thy ougly shamelesness, and shalt onely perceive him to have bene a Creator in thy destruction" (410). Thus, she brings the argument full circle with her return to tight parallelism reminiscent of the exordium.

The other speeches illustrating Pamela's magnificent, just disdain also show evidence of Sidney's careful control of structure to illustrate a character's controlling principle. Pamela's second contemptuous response to Cecropia begins with the command "followe one, doo what thou wilt and canst" (472), then turns on the contrast of the verbs wilt and canst to inform the rest of the speech. The princess first acknowledges what Cecropia wills and has the ability to do, then explains what she would but cannot do: Cecropia can destroy Pamela's body, but she cannot destroy her heart. Pamela's reply to Amphialus achieves unity through its controlling parallelism and suspension.

Following a contemptuous vocative, the speech falls into three distinct sections, each introduced by an imperative. Each section becomes somewhat longer than the previous one, with the last interrupted by two qualifying clauses, thus suspending Pamela's final insult. Finally, Pamela rejects Anaxius's offer of marriage with a series of antithetical nouns. The pairs are complementary, but the order of the third and final pair is reversed: comedy/tragedy, life/death, hangman/husband. The antitheses both order the speech and ironically emphasize the insult: "Proud beast (said she) yet thou plainest worse thy Comedy than thy Tragedy. For my part, assure thy selfe, since my destiny is such, that at each moment my life and death stand in equall balance, I had rather have thee, and think thee far fitter to be my hangman, than my husband."

In contrast, Philoclea never speaks in anger; rather her speeches illustrate the essential sweetness and humility of gentle beauty. One speech of Philoclea's shows similarities to Pamela's disdainful speeches but is quite different in tone and style and thus shows the contrast between the constitutive qualities of Majesty and Beauty. Amphialus approaches Philoclea with an apology for the inequities she has suffered. Before Philoclea speaks, Sidney directs our attention to her conduct and describes her demeanor as sorrowful, without kindness but displaying no anger. Philoclea responds to Amphialus with a speech possessing a formal unity reminiscent of Pamela's disdainful speeches. After addressing him, Philoclea begins with a statement of paradox: "What shall my tongue be able to doo, which is infourmed by the eares one way, and by the eyes another?" (368). This paradox is followed by five examples of contradictions between what she perceives as Amphialus's behavior and what she hears him promise. Each example is presented in parallel, balanced clauses. The second section of her speech contains two sentences, each having the structure conditional clause plus resultant clause. This structure plus the conjunction "but" which links the two sentences, emphasizes the resultant clause. For example:

> If then violence, injurie, terror, and depriving of that which is more dear than life it selfe, libertie, be fit orators for affection, you may expect that I will be easily perswaded. But if the nearenesse of our kindred breede any remorse in you, or there be any such thing in you, which you call love towarde me, then let not my fortune be disgraced with the name of imprisonment: let not my hart waste it selfe by being vexed with feeling evill, and fearing worse. (368–69)

This speech, like Pamela's, exhibits a control of emotions through its tight structure. Pamela's speech, however, demonstrates controlled anger, whereas Philoclea's shows controlled sorrow. She addresses Amphialus with the simple "cousin," a vocative that suggests none of the contempt expressed by Pamela in similar situations. Further, all Philoclea's imperatives are tempered by the auxiliary "let," which creates a tone more of persuasion than command; in addition, she never expresses contempt with the second-person singular pronoun. Finally, the syntax is simple and unadorned. Thus, the structure of Philoclea's response to Amphialus recalls the form of Pamela's speeches of anger, whereas the tone, as expressed by the vocative, modified imperatives, and choice of personal pronoun, is significantly different and consequently distinguishes the two philosophical types. Indeed, in the same way that

Pamela's speeches of just disdain establish her character as a philosophical type, Philoclea's speeches illustrate the essential sweetness
and humility of her philosophical type.

Philoclea's speeches to Pyrocles throughout also show her sweetness. Unlike the relationship of Pamela and Musidorus, Philoclea
and Pyrocles are quite intimate by virtue of Pyrocles' disguise as a
woman. Because of this early intimacy, when Pyrocles reveals his
true identity, their previously established closeness allows Philoclea
the freedom to speak informally. Of this speech, Arthur Amos has
argued that Philoclea's "unusually awkward and choppy syntax
reflects the disturbance Pyrocles' revelation has created on Philoclea's mind" (140). Although Amos is right that the speech begins
with choppy syntax, it progresses to a series of controlled rhetorical
questions that show her gradual acceptance of her condition, and
ends with a sweet expression of her love and a plea for his mercy:
"Thou hast then the victorie: use it with vertue. Thy vertue wan me;
with vertue preserve me. Doost thou love me: keepe me then still
worthy to be beloved" (260–61). Thus, the syntax of the final three
sentences, with their parallelism and antithesis, illustrates her re-
newed control.

Perhaps more than any other speech, Philoclea's lament for her
sister exemplifies the essence of Beauty.[15] Unlike Pamela, who
generally intellectualizes experience, Philoclea responds in a personal way. The speech is composed of ten sentences, the first and
last exhibiting inverted-order syntactic form. She begins by addressing her sister with the chiastic "Pamela my sister, my sister Pamela"
(477) and ends with two parallel questions, both in inverted order.
The first follows the structure subject-verb-adverb/adverb-verb-
subject, and the second follows a somewhat looser form of subject-
verb-adjective, complement/verb-subject: "But thou arte gone,
and where am I? Pamela is dead; and live I?" (478). In addition
to this syntactic parallelism, the speech's first and last sentences
are semantically parallel as well, a characteristic extended to the
second and penultimate sentences. The stylistic form mirrors the
semantic. Philoclea begins and ends with her sorrow at living without her sister, then this expression of sorrow is followed in the beginning and preceded at the end by amplification. Each sentence
repeats the adverb "nevermore" to signify her grief that not only
does death separate her from her sister, but that the separation is
irrevocable. This point is illustrated in the second sentence: "Pamela never more shall I see the: never more shall I enjoy thy sweet
company, and wise counsell" (477), and in the ninth sentence:
"Never more shall I lie with thee: never more shall we bathe in

the pleasant river together; never more shall I see thee in thy shephearde apparell" (478).

The tightness and economy of the outer structure bracket six rather long sentences. Unlike her style when recounting tales, this passage contains little interruption or suspension. Each clause begins with a short syntactic unit followed by a longer unit expanded by means of auxiliary verbs or modification by word or phrase. The only conjunctions between clauses join parallel clauses—no transitions are used between parallel units. The effect is a dirgelike cadence that shows the intensity of Philoclea's anguish; thus, syntax and form, joined with content, exemplify the sweet virtue of sorrow.

Finally, two speeches in a similar mode demonstrate the contrast between the exemplars of Majesty and Beauty. Both speeches are prayers, but their contexts are quite different. Philoclea prays for guidance when she fears that she loves a woman; Pamela prays for strength when she faces death. A comparison of the two speeches shows the ways that Sidney contrasts the characters both by the roles they play and the philosophical ideas they represent. Pamela's role never places her in a paradoxical situation quite like that of Philoclea. Generally, she understands the events occurring around her because true Majesty is associated with reasoning. Although she must dress and act as a shepherdess, she understands her predictment and even when imprisoned is never confused. Because Beauty is associated with intuition, Philoclea often expresses her faith and sweet acceptance in the face of her lack of understanding. Her prayer for guidance illustrates both her confusion at loving a woman and her final acceptance despite her confusion. Throughout the speech, her diction, syntax, and form demonstrate her personal response. Pamela responds to her situation with her mind, whereas Philoclea responds with her senses. Pamela explains her imprisonment with abstract nouns such as misery, chastizement, bondage, and affliction, whereas Philoclea uses concrete nouns such as torment and plague.

In addition, a contrast of light and dark images represents the conflict Philoclea feels. She sees events that appear to contradict her prior understanding, and her confusion becomes the cloud that obstructs the light of her virtue. Her vocatives in particular illustrate her lack of comprehension. Although Pamela repeatedly addresses her Lord, Philoclea first addresses herself, then Diana, the stars, herself again, love, and, finally, Zelmane. Further, although Pamela presents her prayer in a succession of parallel clauses with transitions marking her shift from one series of parallel clauses to the next, Philoclea's speech is loosely structured and characterized by a lack of transitions. In addition, she shifts from a series of questions to two extremely hypotactic sentences, interrupted by several modifying clauses, to a series of tightly parallel clauses, to a series of short questions, and on to her final pair of brief, understated sentences that are notable for their clarity after the complex sentences of the rest of the passage.

Two brief passages from the two speeches illustrate the differences in style. Both passages rely heavily on parallel structure—both repeating parallel components and variation to display the character's condition and the crescendo of emotional intensity. In the passage from Pamela's prayer, Sidney emphasizes the majesty of her acceptance of the will of God. In the passage from Philoclea's soliloquy, the parallelism suggests first her acceptance of and then resistance to her situation:

Pamela: But yet my God if in thy wisdom, this be the aptest chastizement from my inexcusable follie; if this low bondage be fittest for my overhie desires; if the pride of my not-inough humble harte, be thus to be broken, O lord I yeeld unto thy will (383).

Philoclea: If it be so, then (O you Stars) judge rightly of me, and if I have with wicked intent made my selfe a pray to fancie, or if by any idle lustes I framed my harte fit for such an impression, then let this plague dayly increase in me, till my name bee made odious to womankind. But if extreame and unresistable violence have oppressed me, who will ever do any of you sacrifice (O you Starres) if you do not succour me? (174)

This example from Pamela's prayer, with its three parallel conditional clauses balanced by the central copula "be," suggests an epistemological position that explains her inevitable movement to an acceptance of faith. The subjects of the conditional clauses vary from "this" to "this low bondage" to "the pride of my not-inough humble harte." This variation echoes the variation in the subject complement in the previous clause and thus demonstrates the logical progression of the idea. "This low bondage" of the second clause is the specific punishment implied by the "chastizement" in the previous clause. Likewise, "pride" in the third clause explains the "overhie" desires in the second clause. Although using such grammatical parallelism, however, Sidney shifts out of semantic parallelism with the third clause. The subject of the third clause is not a true variant of the first two, which refer to Pamela's imprisonment. In addition, the copula of the third clause is extended with the passive infinitive "to be broken." This break in semantic parallelism has the effect of completing Pamela's self-evaluation and thus leading to her final clause of resignation. The vocatives vary from the intimate "my God" to the formal "O Lord," which bracket the three parallel clauses; the change emphasizes the completion of her self-analysis. Thus, the passage moves to the resignation and faith of the eloquent "I yeeld to thy will."

Philoclea's soliloquy demonstrates the way the same techniques achieve a rather different effect. The passage contains three series of parallel clauses, each following the form of conditional clause plus resultant clause. The middle section recalls both the structure and tone of Pamela's parallel conditional clauses. In this section, however, no growth of understanding is signaled by a shift in the structure of the clauses—the two clauses are synonymous. In this passage, Sidney uses a contrast between sections to demonstrate Philoclea's confusion. The third section exhibits a change in the parallelism. The pattern of the second section, verb plus reflexive pronoun, is contrasted by the verb plus personal pronoun of the third section. Concurrently, the subject shifts in the conditional clause of the third section to an external, abstract force that contrasts with the first-person pronoun. A similar shift occurs in the main clauses from the imperatives, "judge rightly of me" and "let this plague dayly increase in me," to the plaintive question "who will ever do any of you sacrifice (O you Starres) if you do not succour me?" These structural and semantic changes have an effect similar to the semantic shift in Pamela's passage. Although the variation in Pamela's syntax illustrates a growth in understanding, however, that in Philoclea's shows her essential confusion and doubt. Thus, the differences in the speech patterns of the two passages demonstrate the differences both in context and in type.

Although it might appear that by matching style to individual, Sidney is creating characters with psychological depth and thus foreshadowing the development of characters in the novel, an observation made by at least one critic,[16] his notion of character is rather more complex. Like Malory, Sidney distinguishes between parallel characters by the roles they play in the plot. Yet Sidney's vision of character is rather different from Malory's. Sidney's characters are at once types defined by social position and types identified by philosophical virtue. The concept of character is further complicated by the fact that Sidney sometimes chooses episodes in the plot to illustrate a particular aspect of a philosophical type, whereas at other times he maintains the similarities of characters of the same societal type. Although he suggests the real world in his portrayal of characters as representatives of their social class, the portrayal is of a class, not an individual. Further, although he represents the psychology of the human experience, the experience is of a philosophical ideal, not an individual. Finally, although he presents human experiences that possess logical development and require characters consonant with the plot, the human experience is a universal one in an idealized romance setting. In the *New Arcadia*, then, we find characters who seem at times to be unique, individualized characters whose speech patterns often display their individual qualities. Nonetheless, because their manners of speaking change according to the effect Sidney is attempting rather than according to any internal consistency, they remain, though multidimensional, typed characters, not the consistent, idiosyncratic characters of the novel.

4

The Conflict of World Views in *Wuthering Heights*

Although considered to be one of the most idiosyncratic works in the history of English fiction,[1] *Wuthering Heights* reflects many of the changes in the mainstream concept of character. Colin Wilson, in his "A Personal Response to *Wuthering Heights*," reminds us that Emily Brontë wrote her work in the century following the publication of Samuel Richardson's *Pamela*, which in many ways, with its exploration of a young woman's imagination, marked a turning point in techniques of characterization. By the time Emily Brontë wrote *Wuthering Heights*, Wilson observes, individualization of characters, even minor ones, was well established as a characteristic of a good novel. Yet Brontë seems concerned with far more than just writing a good mimetic novel. With her interest in principles and metaphysical forces, she also is working within the tradition of the crafted romance, a genre much in vogue in the late eighteenth and early nineteenth centuries.[2]

In crafted romances, individuation was still subordinate to type. The speeches in *Wuthering Heights* show the influence of both traditions. Although its characters have more developed, consistent individual qualities than in either *Le Morte Darthur* or *New Arcadia*, they are types nonetheless. Although functioning in ways rather different from the characters in Malory's or Sidney's romances, they also represent principles seen working in the text. In Brontë's work, characters' consistent diction shows them to be both individuals and types. Working within these traditions, Brontë uses paradigms in dialogue to illustrate philosophical principles that result from the meeting of a psychological type and a particular environment. Further, each character remains essentially the same throughout the work and thus they can be seen as closed, paradigmatic characters, to use Chatman's terminology.[3] By isolating principles as represented by basically static individuals, Brontë subordinates individuation of characters to her particular controlling idea. The result, it seems to me, is a work of fiction that focuses more on the conflict of the principles expressed by its characters and their voices than on an exploration of the psychology of individual characters.

As most readers have observed, *Wuthering Heights* presents two generations of parallel love triangles, highlighting in each the female characters: in the first generation, Catherine Earnshaw, and in the second, her daughter Cathy Linton. In addition to creating the parallel plot lines, Brontë makes both women the same general psychological type—strong willed, somewhat selfish, impetuous, spirited, and, to varying degrees, blind to the implications of their decisions. As children, both are mischievous and energetic. Nelly Dean's descriptions of the young Catherine and Cathy explain their similarities as types. Of Catherine, she says:

> Certainly, she had ways with her such as I never saw a child take up before; and she put all of us past our patience fifty times and oftener in a day: from the hour she came downstairs, till the hour she went to bed, we had not a minute's security that she wouldn't be in mischief. Her spirits were always at high-water mark, her tongue always going— singing, laughing, and plaguing everybody who would not do the same. A wild wicked slip she was—but she had the bonniest eye and sweetest smile, and lightest foot in the parish; and after all, I believe she meant no harm; for when once she made you cry in good earnest, it seldom happened that she would not keep you company, and oblige you to be quiet that you might comfort her.[4]

Of Cathy, she says:

> She was the most winning thing that ever brought sunshine into a desolate house—a real beauty in face, with the Earnshaw's handsome dark eyes, but the Linton's fair skin, and small features, and yellow curling hair. Her spirit was high, though not rough, and qualified by a heart sensitive and lively to excess in its affections. That capacity for intense attachments reminded me of her mother; still she did not resemble her, for she could be soft and mild as a dove, and she had a gentle voice, and pensive expression: her anger was never furious; her love never fierce; it was deep and tender.
>
> However, it must be acknowledged, she had faults to foil her gifts. A propensity to be saucy was one; and a perverse will that indulged children invariably acquire, whether they be good tempered or cross. (155)

In addition to implying their similarities, of course, Nelly Dean's descriptions indicate the essential differences between mother and daughter. Although representing similar psychological types, Catherine Earnshaw and her daughter Cathy reflect the worlds of their births and early childhoods. Each child seems indigenous to her environment and symbolically equated with the vegetation natural to each region. Like the hardy firs that survive in the windswept vicinity of Wuthering Heights, Catherine is the dark-haired, dark-eyed child of storm. Cathy, though an offspring of the stern and fierce Earnshaws, is more like the honeysuckles associated with the gentler climate of Thrushcross Grange. She is fair-skinned and light-haired, and although she has the dark eyes and impetuous nature of her mother, her temperament is milder. As Nelly explains, "her anger was never furious; her love never fierce; it was deep and tender" (155).

In addition to representing the essence of her natural environment, each character illustrates the effects of growing up in such an environment. Catherine was raised in an environment of storm, wind, and deprivation, which stunted, twisted, and bent the natural growth of trees in the yard where she played. The strict and rigid father she loved repeatedly rejected her affection, and although his rejections initially caused her pain, eventually they hardened her. In contrast, her daughter thrived in a shimmering world of light and comfort. Her father indulged and educated Cathy without ever speaking a harsh word to her; consequently, Cathy is more pliant and reasonable than her mother. The interaction between the general psychological type and the qualities attributable to environmental influences creates parallel but individuated characters. Her natural energy repressed, Catherine is excessive, violent, and passionate; her daughter, fondly nurtured and supported, is a more moderate reflection of her mother. The difference is, as Miriam Allott has observed, that the second generation modifies the intensity of the first by having an energy "more normal and human."[5]

The contrast, however, is more than merely between violence and normal energy. As Dorothy Van Ghent notes, Emily Brontë presents two kinds of reality, two world views, one raw and almost inhuman, the other civilized. The tension, Dorothy Van Ghent continues, "between these two kinds of reality, their inveterate opposition and at the same time their *continuity* one with another, provides at once the content and the form of *Wuthering Heights*."[6] Although Van Ghent's comment refers to the differences between the two houses rather than specifically to mother and daughter, the observation can be extended to illustrate the differences between the two main female characters. Much as the two houses represent the competing realities throughout the book, each woman repeatedly demonstrates her vision of reality in nearly every speech she utters. For all her wildly passionate, apparently willful statements, Catherine sees the world controlled by forces beyond her will. As early as her first return from Thrushcross Grange, Catherine tells Heathcliff, "I did not mean to laugh at you. . . . I could not hinder myself" (52) as if she believes her actions divinely decreed. She also frequently attributes her state of mind as well as her actions to the power of some exterior force. She says at various points, "I've no power of be merry" (99); later, "I am pushed to extremity" (101); and finally, "I had no command of tongue or brain" (107).

In contrast, Cathy sees the world as a dynamic place, subject to the will of the people who inhabit it. Unlike her mother, who repeatedly avows her faith in the authority of a higher truth, Cathy asserts her independence from authority and relies on reasoning. She explains to Nelly, "I can get over the wall. . . . The Grange is not a prison, Ellen, and you are not my jailer. And besides, I'm almost seventeen. I'm a woman" (195). Even when Heathcliff forces her to marry young Linton, she asserts her independence by qualifying her acquiescence: "I'll marry him, within this hour, if I may go to Thrushcross Grange afterwards" (219). Because Emily Brontë draws attention to the similar patterns in the two stories, and, as we shall see shortly, to the parallel patterns of speech as well, she sets them dialectically opposite.

Both Dorothy Van Ghent and Mark Schorer, in his influential article "Fiction and the 'Analogical Matrix,'"[7] have recognized the way the diction of *Wuthering Heights* exemplifies the excesses and power of the first generation. Neither, however, extends the analysis to discuss how Emily Brontë illustrates the vision of what Van Ghent has called the "finite world,"[8] the world of Cathy Linton, in *her* language—yet exploiting the language differential of the two parallel characters is one of the significant ways Emily Brontë contrasts the opposing realities of her work. Despite their similarities, mother and daughter are quite different; Brontë define that difference, at least in part, by assigning particular, unique speech patterns to each. They differ both in their inherent qualities and in their environmentally imposed characteristics. One way Emily Brontë creates the differences between them is through individuated speech patterns that represent the two conflicting world views Van Ghent has suggested as the content and the form of *Wuthering Heights*.

Several critics have seen the differences between the two characters reflected in their speech patterns. John E. Jordon, for instance, has argued that although Cathy's speeches are often almost ludicrous parallels to her mother's, her words demonstrate a richer perception.[9] Helene Moglen finds evidence in dialogue for her position that Catherine's speeches reflect the selfish passions of a child, whereas those of her daughter represent the emotional maturity of the self and generosity of a woman.[10] Similarly, John Beverslius contends that Catherine's speech patterns psychologically reveal her lack of self-knowledge.[11] Also sympathetic to the portrayal of the young Cathy, William Madden argues that her speeches show her capacity to evaluate her emotions honestly.[12] In contrast, David Sonstroem asserts that the diction of the speeches show all the characters to have limited viewpoints.[13] Furthermore, Arnold Krupat argues that none of the main characters has fixed, consistent diction, and, as a result, "we have no reliable word from anyone in the book as to how to take it."[14] All of these readings, as perceptive as they are, however, stop short of closely examining the carefully crafted contrasting patterns of speech and the rhetorical implications of these patterns.

To contrast the two styles, Emily Brontë sets them parallel by emphasizing the similarities of the two characters' speech patterns in the overall syntactic characteristics of their discourse. Their average sentence lengths, for example, differ very little. In addition, each one's sentences lengthen as she matures, so that their averages are quite similar, both as children and as young women. Furthermore, each character uses much longer sentences when narrating events, and, again, their averages are very close.[15] With the parallels set, Brontë is able to make a clear distinction between the two styles.

The most obvious difference is in their diction. Mark Schorer has argued that Brontë's diction is passionate, her verbs violent, and "everything is at a pitch from which it can only subside."[16] Although Schorer's description certainly applies to Catherine's diction, it fails to account for the milder words of her daughter. Cathy's verbs, for example, can be intense; yet although she often uses the same verbs as Catherine such as sobbed, wept, destroy, detest, despise, degrade, drawn, tumble, and endure, Cathy never reaches the level of intensity, the full-blown violent passion expressed by Catherine's other verbs such as tormented, haunted, burning, beating, dashed, seize, devour, and annihilated.

Similarly, Catherine's modifiers amplify their head words, and Cathy's are less extreme. Catherine does not call Linton's blood merely cold, but says his veins are "full of ice water" (101); Heathcliff is not merely fierce and cruel, but he is a "pitiless, wolfish man" (90). Blackness is "utter blackness" (107); oblivion is "eternal oblivion" (92); and gratitude is "blind ingratitude" (99). Cathy, at the height of her anger, calls Heathcliff "miserable" and "lonely like the devil" (228), Hareton a "brute" (191), and Linton a "little liar" (192). Unlike her mother who intensifies nouns and adjectives as she does in "bitter misery" (87), "raging mad," "wickedly ungrateful" (107), and "extremely miserable" (72), Cathy typically moderates through modifiers as in "hardly understood" (179), "quite cordial" (180), "very truth" (197), and "generally stayed" (198). One modifier in particular illustrates the difference. "Little" appears only twice in Catherine's speeches and both times in a contemptuous description of Isabella. To belittle her sister-in-law, Catherine describes her as an "impertinent little monkey" (89) and later as her "poor little sister-in-law" (91). Cathy, conversely, uses the adjective frequently but only once in a pejorative or contemptuous manner when she calls Linton a "little liar" (192). Other times the adjective is an affectionate diminutive as in "pretty little Linton" (191) or as a persuasive technique by which she suggests the moderation of her requests. She asks Nelly, for example, "May we not go a little way—half a mile, Ellen, only just half a mile?" (163). In addition, when Cathy tries to reason Linton out of a tantrum brought on by her giving his chair an angry push, she tells him, "But I couldn't have been hurt by that little push" (193). Finally, when she attempts to win Hareton's forgiveness, she says, "Say you forgive me, Hareton, do! You can make me so happy, by speaking that little word" (248).

The differences in diction illustrate and contrast the two world views. Not only does Catherine use excessive language but she also catagorizes, labels, and judges with absolute certainty. By doing so, she exhibits her vision of reality as one with clearly delineated and separate absolutes, elements, and principles. Her universe is a predetermined, relentless, cosmic puzzle. In contrast, Cathy's diction shows her more "civilized" view. For her, the universe allows choice. With her careful qualifiers she nods to her listener and thus acknowledges the possibility of compromise and the necessity of persuasion.

The rhetoric of their sentences, notably in their hypothetical statements, commands, and requests, also demonstrates the differences between mother and daughter. Two basic syntactic structures for hypothetical statements are common to both. The first links a conditional or concessive clause containing the hypothetical subjunctive were or quasi-subjunctive (had or should, for example) with a main clause containing either should or would. Using the hypothetical subjunctive, Cathy says, "I'd make such a pet of him, if he were mine," (195) and, with the quasi-subjunctive, Catherine says, "Should the meanest thing alive slap me on the cheek, I'd not only turn the other, but I'd ask pardon for provoking it" (87). In the second structure, a subordinate clause containing the subjunctive follows an optative verb such as wish, as in "I wish I were out of doors" (107).

Despite their similarity in pattern, the hypothetical statements of the two characters differ subtly and in doing so reflect the contrast in ideologies. Catherine uses the subjunctive more than twice as often as her daughter. In nearly half of her subjunctives, Catherine chooses the auxiliary should rather than would in the main clause, frequently when she is the subject. The choice reinforces her assertions of the inevitability of her actions, the should implying either obligation or logical necessity.[17] For example, when justifying her decision to marry Edgar Linton she tells Nelly, "if the wicked man in there had not brought Heathcliff so low, I shouldn't have thought of it" (72). Likewise, before narrating her dream of heaven, she says, "If I were in heaven, Nelly, I should be extremely miserable" (72). Later, when she is ill, she declares, "I'm sure I should be myself were I once among the heather on those hills" (107). In each statement, the word should implies obligation rather than volition. When she considers her future, she concludes that some external force requires her to marry Edgar and be miserable in heaven but well in the climate of Wuthering Heights.

Cathy clearly lacks this belief in inevitability. Unlike her mother, she employs the modal should in fewer than one-quarter of all subjunctives and only once when she is the subject. She tells Hareton, "I should like you to be my cousin now, if you had not grown so cross to me, and so rough" (247). Despite the quasi-subjunctive had, the form is really a modification of the idiom appropriate to a main verb of preference, a form she employs frequently to express desire, not to imply inevitability.[18] Other than this one instance, in all other cases of the subjunctive in which she might have chosen "I should," she elects instead "I would" or the ambiguous "I'd." One such situation, in particular, illustrates the way the alternate form defines a difference in world view.[19] Trapped against her will at Wuthering Heights, Cathy turns to Heathcliff and, in a voice and manner that reminds him of her mother, scornfully tells hims, "I wouldn't eat or drink here, if I were starving" (215). Despite the similarity to her mother in voice and manner, Cathy relies on the modal would, which Brontë uses to make an important distinction between the characters. Although both mother and daughter are willful, Cathy makes choices. She chooses not to eat, whereas her mother most certainly would have accepted the inevitability of not eating.

The characters' commands also show Brontë highlighting the differences between them. Although both use imperatives extensively, Cathy tends to employ them more often in a persuasive manner and by doing so demonstrates her faith in the power of reasoning. Catherine's imperatives, conversely, are clearly commands—indeed ones given without any justification beyond the implicit "because she desires it." By issuing commands, Catherine implies a faith in her inherent right to expect acquiescence. She commands Nelly to leave the room when Edgar comes courting; she requires Edgar to remain when he wishes to leave; she orders her husband to fight Heathcliff or to apologize for insulting him. None of these commands contains a reason.

In addition to issuing commands without qualification or justification, Catherine often strengthens her imperatives by retaining the subject you, issuing a type of command that Quirk and Greenbaum characterize as "usually admonitory in tone, and expressing strong irritation,"[20] She makes these commands even more emphatic by her modal auxiliary of obligation, shall, or compulsion, must. When Edgar attempts to leave her, for example, she insists, "you must not go . . . you shall not leave" (66). When Heathcliff returns after his long absence, Catherine emphatically informs Linton, "You must be friends now" (83). After tormenting Isabella, Catherine refuses to allow her to escape, insisting, "you sha'n't run off . . . you shall stay" (92). Then mocking Isabella's attempt to extricate herself by force, she warns Heathcliff, "you must beware of your eyes" (92–93). Later, however, she tempers her cruelty to Isabella, telling Heathcliff, "you must let Isabella alone" (97). Finally, in her last words to Heathcliff, she says, "You must not go . . . you shall not" (135). In each case, the combination of imperative subject and modal auxiliary of obligation or compulsion insists on the obligatory response.

In a somewhat softer vein, Catherine on occasion requests help with an imploring imperative, but her accompanying actions insistently require the desired response. Two instances illustrate the way she combines an imploring imperative with a commanding physical action. First, she begs Nelly to open the window so that she might be revived by a wind from the Heights: "Do let me fell it—it comes straight down the moor—Do let me have one breath" (106). In her final meeting with Heathcliff, she implores him to come to her with the insistent "Do come to me Heathcliff" (134). In both instances, her actions demand a response—in the first her voice threatens madness while she wrings her hands, thus requiring Nelly to pacify her by satisfying her request. In the second, she rises and falls toward Heathcliff, thus requiring him to catch her.

The only times Catherine justifies her commands, her explanation generally implies that her demand must be obeyed simply because she insists on her will being met. Her explanation of the ways she persuades Heathcliff is typical of her attempts to convince everyone: "I never say to him, 'Let this or that enemy alone, because it would be ungenerous or cruel to harm them'; I say, 'Let them alone, because *I* should hate them to be wronged'" (90). Thus, when she commands Edgar not to leave her, she explains that she would be miserable all night if he did; when she orders Joseph to be silent, she explains that she does not wish any insolence in her presence; and when she tells Edgar that he and Heathcliff must be friends, it is for her sake.

Cathy's commands differ markedly from her mother's. In fact, only a few of her imperatives are clearly commands. The infrequent instances include her commanding Hareton to make haste and get her horse; telling Nelly that she must not reveal their encounter with Heathcliff to her father; requiring Linton to release her; demanding that Heathcliff relinquish the key he holds so she might escape; and scornfully ordering Hareton to leave her alone. Although these instances seem frequent, the number of commands pales in comparison with the occurrences in her mother's discourse. Further, Cathy's imperative voice seems a distant echo of her mother's, but the tone is quite different.

Although she sometimes employs the imperative plus subject form, Cathy rarely links it with a modal auxiliary of obligation. In fact, she uses the form only two times: once when she addresses Nelly and once with her cousin Linton. Although she is insistent in both instances, she adds reasons for her listeners to obey her. She tells Nelly, "You must hold your tongue about my uncle: he's *my* uncle, remember, and I'll scold papa for quarrelling with him" (179). To Linton, she says, "Yes, Linton; you must tell. It was for your sake I came; and it will be wickedly ungrateful if you refuse" (216). Brontë consistently maintains a distinction between the two character's imperatives: Catherine selects the form to assert authority, whereas Cathy tempers it with reasoning. In addition, Catherine clearly commands, whereas Cathy more often petitions. She implores, "don't let them say such things"; later, "O, give them to me"; and, most emphatically, "Oh, put them in the fire, do, do!"

The two characters differ also in their interrogative sentences, and the distinctions are analogous to those seen in their commands. Catherine generally implies commands with her questions, whereas Cathy's questions most often are supplications. In Catherine's confession that she loves Heathcliff but will marry Edgar, for example, she begins with what appears to be a supplication: "Nelly, will you keep a secret for me?" (70). In her next sentence, however, she reveals her true intention to confess her secret whether or not Nelly wishes to hear: "it worries me, and I must let it out!" (70). Later, when Heathcliff first reappears after his long absence, Catherine ostensibly asks permission to invite him into the parlor, but when Edgar suggests the kitchen as a more suitable spot, she shows that what appeared a request was, in actuality, a demand: "No, . . . I cannot sit in the kitchen" (84). Similarly, after Edgar and Heathcliff quarrel, Catherine demands that Nelly tell Edgar that his actions have distressed her, and that, as a result, she is in danger of becoming ill. She ends her demands with an imploring: "Will you do so, my good Nelly?" Yet her tone is clearly demanding, and she does not, for a moment, doubt that Nelly will obey her.

Cathy's requests, conversely, are clearly supplications. She repeatedly requests information or favors with questions. When she first encounters her cousin Hareton, for instance, she mistakenly thinks him a servant. Puzzled by his angry response to her demands, she turns to Nelly for an explanation: "How dare he speak so to me? Mustn't he be made to do as I ask him?" (160). Further, forbidden to visit Wuthering Heights and her cousin Linton, she begs Nelly, "But may I not write a note to tell him why I cannot come. . . And just send those books I promised to lend him? His books are not as nice as mine, and he wanted to have them extremely, when I told him how interesting they were. May I not, Ellen?" (181). The questions attempt to persuade Nelly to comply; yet although they may be examples of subterfuge, and thus manipulative, they do not demand her acquiescence. Later after an argument with Linton, she repeatedly implores him to let her remain and make amends: "'Must I go?'" asked Catherine dolefully, bending over him. "'Do you want me to go, Linton?'" "'You can't alter what you've done,'" he replied pettishly, shrinking from her, "'unless you alter it for the worse, by teasing me into a fever.'" "'Well, then I must go'" (193). Eventually called back by her petulant cousin, she ingratiatingly asks, "And you want me—you would wish to see me sometimes, really?" Finally, after narrating her clandestine visits to Wuthering Heights, she implores Nelly not to tell her father and attempts to give reasons Nelly should grant her request: "Now, Ellen, you have heard all; and I can't be prevented from going to Wuthering Heights, except by inflicting misery on two people; whereas, if you'll only not tell papa, my going need disturb the tranquillity of none. You'll not tell, will you? It will be very heartless of you if you do" (204). Although her tone is insistent, her question is a request, a supplication, rather than a demand.

Thus, although there are basic, structural similarities in the two characters' hypothetical statements, imperatives, and interrogatives, subtle differences remain. The contrast between Catherine's demanding tone and Cathy's more persuasive tone suggests a fundamental difference in their world views. Catherine knows how she would certainly act in any hypothetical situation because she believes her response to be determined by her very nature, and her subjunctives illustrate this belief in absolutes. Further, she believes she has a natural authority, which gives her the right to make demands of others without justifying or persuading; as a result, her imperatives are insistent and demanding. In contrast, Cathy's world is one of logical consequence. Although Catherine seems moved either by forces beyond her or by her faith in such forces, Cathy has the ability to make choices. Thus, her subjunctives express volition, and her imperatives and interrogatives acknowledge the volition of others.

The structure of their longer speeches also illustrates this difference in their perspectives. Catherine most often uses a short period, and few transitions or unifying devices. When she does achieve a kind of unity, it is by repeating or paraphrasing her assertions, rarely by demonstrating logical relationships. Her attempts to move people are mere reminders of her authority to issue orders and expect acquiescence. Cathy's speeches, by comparison, have a kind of argumentative strategy—she attempts to move her listener with persuasion rather than authority. Her periods are longer, often connected by parallel structure and conjunctions indicating their logical relationships. A comparison of two representative speeches on similar themes illustrates the differences. Shortly before her death, Catherine questions Heathcliff's love, saying:

> I wish I could hold you . . . till we were both dead! I shouldn't care what you suffered. I care nothing for your sufferings. Why shouldn't you suffer? I do! Will you forgive me—will you be happy when I am in the earth? Will you say twenty years hence, "That's the grave of Catherine Earnshaw. I loved her long ago, and was wretched to lose her; but it is past. I've loved many others since—my children are dearer to me than she was, and, at death, I shall not rejoice that I am going to her, I shall be sorry that I must leave them!" Will you say so, Heathcliff? (133)

In a speech that John E. Jordan notes as parallel to the elder Catherine's rebuke of Heathcliff (10), Cathy tells Heathcliff:

> I know he has a bad nature . . . he's your son. But I'm glad I've a better, to forgive it; and I know he loves me and for that reason I love him. Mr. Heathcliff, *you* have *nobody* to love you; and, however miserable you make us, we shall still have the revenge of thinking that your cruelty rises

from your greater misery! you are miserable, are you not? Lonely, like the devil, and envious like him? *Nobody* loves you—*nobody* will cry for you, when you die! I wouldn't be you! (228)

To unify her speech, Catherine repeats and paraphrases with slight variation in meaning, and yet her speech is disjointed, lacking in any logical progression. The first five sentences are tonally joined as each reminds Heathcliff of his agony and informs him that she does not wish to hold him to cause him suffering but simply because of her own desires. She questions his love throughout the speech without giving any reasons for her doubt and, in fact, without any logical links between thoughts. The periods are short without transition, their only links in the tonal unity created by the repeated words. Cathy, however, shows the logical connections in her speech. In the first half, she uses conjunctions and transitions including "but," "and," and "for that reason." In the second half, she seems initially to follow the pattern of her mother's speech, repeating either the main word or idea from the previous sentence. Unlike her mother, though, Cathy's repeated terms underline a progression of thought as she extends her analysis of his misery. She moves from her observation that Heathcliff has no one to love him to his own misery and the attributes of his misery. Thus, the repeated words show the logical development of her argument. By the end, she has earned the right to conclude scornfully, "I wouldn't be you!"

A comparison of speeches in similar contexts further illustrates the ways Emily Brontë uses form, syntax, and diction to differentiate the two world views. Three speeches of Cathy's in particular echo speeches of Catherine's. In the first pair of speeches, mother and daughter describe their ideas of heaven. Catherine describes a dream she had of being flung from heaven back to Wuthering Heights, her paradise, and Cathy tells of a quarrel she had with her cousin Linton concerning the most perfect paradise. Both Catherine and Cathy contrast their vision of paradise with antithetical views, and their intense, energetic perspectives with relatively passive ones. Catherine sets in opposition an essence of lightning and fire with one of moonbeam and frost; Cathy contrasts an ecstacy of dance and jubilee with a vision of peace and serenity. In other ways, the two speeches differ, however. Catherine's speech reveals her faith in absolutes with its polarized opposites, whereas Cathy's expresses an acceptance of shared values. Although Catherine's opposites are mutually exclusive, Cathy's admit overlap. Catherine tells Nelly:

This is nothing. . . . I was only going to say that heaven did not seem to be my home; and I broke my heart with weeping to come back to earth;

and the angels were so angry that they flung me out, into the middle of the heath on the top of Wuthering Heights; where I woke sobbing for joy. That will do to explain my secret, as well as the other. I've no more business to marry Edgar Linton than I have to be in heaven; and if the wicked man in there had not brought Heathcliff so low, I shouldn't have thought of it. It would degrade me to marry Heathcliff now; so he shall never know how I love him; and that, not because he's handsome, Nelly, but because he's more myself than I am. Whatever our souls are made of, his and mine are the same, and Linton's is as different as a moonbeam from lightning, or frost from fire. (72)

Cathy recalls:

One time, however, we were near quarrelling. He said the pleasantest manner of spending a hot July day was lying from morning till evening on a bank of heath in the middle of the moors, with the bees humming dreamily about among the bloom, and the larks singing high up over head, and the blue sky and bright sun shining steadily and cloudlessly. That was his most perfect idea of heaven's happiness. Mine was rocking in a rustling green tree, with a west wind blowing, and bright, white clouds flitting rapidly above; and not only larks, but throstles, and blackbirds, and linnets, and cuckoos pouring out music on every side, and the moors seen at a distance, broken into cool dusky dells; but close by, great swells of long grass undulating in waves to the breeze; and woods and sounding water, and the whole world awake and wild with joy. He wanted all to lie in an ecstacy of peace; I wanted all to sparkle, and dance in a glorious jubilee.

I said his heaven would be only half alive, and he said mine would be drunk; I said I should fall asleep in his, and he said he could not breathe in mine, and began to grow very snappish. At last, we agreed to try both as soon as the right weather came; and then we kissed each other and were friends again. (198–99)

Catherine's speech begins and ends with the conflict of opposites; thus, the structure of the speech supports its pattern of meaning. She begins with the opposition of heaven and heath. Not only is heaven a foreign place for her but also the place that torments and, finally, rejects her. Returned to the heath, she sobs for joy in contrast to her previous sorrowful weeping in exile. Echoing this antithesis, Catherine then associates Edgar with heaven and Heathcliff with the heath. Finally, she extends the contrast by comparing the soul of Edgar to those of Catherine and Heathcliff. No movement toward reconciliation occurs; separation and division are merely repeated in each of the three sections of the speech. In contrast,

Cathy's speech illustrates a progression toward resolution, however tenuous the reconciliation of the final kiss. She begins with extended descriptions of the two opposing views of paradise, then presents a summary of the essential differences of the two views, then an evaluation of each view by the other character, and, finally, a resolution of the conflict as each character is willing to try the other's favorite pastime. The structure of the speech illustrates an openness to reason and the integration of opposing views with its gradual movement from polarities to unity.

The two characters' methods of explanation also differ. Catherine asserts an opposition of elements and in doing so shows her faith in the division of opposites. She gives no description of heaven, or the heath, no reasons why one did not seem to be her home, whereas the other gave her joy. She simply asserts irresolvable differences. Her sentences are declarative statements, each a self-contained assertion without transition, clear pronoun link, or conjunction. With their verbs of being, these declarations demonstrate her metaphysical certainty. Cathy's speech, in contrast, describes the difference between Linton's view heaven and her own. Using indirect discourse, she gives evidence by way of illustration for each viewpoint. She presents each assertion clearly as opinion rather than as incontrovertible fact. Indeed, she specifically identifies each view as an "idea of heaven's happiness" (198). Unlike her mother, she fails to generalize with statements of certainty but moves, in the end, from polarization to a kind of assent: each will try both experiences when summer comes.

Brontë contrasts other speeches of mother and daughter. Cathy's ardent expression of love for her father, for example, echoes her mother's impassioned explanation of her love for Heathcliff. Fearful when her father is ill, Cathy tells Nelly:

> I fret about nothing on earth except papa's illness. I care for nothing in comparison with Papa and I'll never, never—never—never—oh, never, while I have my senses, do any act, or say a word to vex him. I love him better than myself, Ellen; and I know it by this: I pray every night that I may live after him, because I would rather be miserable than he should be—that proves I love him better than myself. (187)

Catherine expresses her love for Heathcliff with:

> I cannot express it; but surely you and everybody have a notion that there is, or should be, an existence of yours beyond you. What were the use of my creation if I were entirely contained here? My great miseries in

this world have been Heathcliff's miseries, and I watched and felt each from the beginning; my great thought in living is himself. If all else perished, and *he* remained, I should still continue to be; and, if all else remained, and he were annihilated, the Universe would turn to a mighty stranger. I should not seem a part of it. My love for Linton is like the foliage in the woods. Time will change it, I'm well aware, as winter changes the trees. My love for Heathcliff resembles the eternal rocks beneath—a source of little visible delight, but necessary. Nelly, I *am* Heathcliff—he's always, always in my mind—not as a pleasure, any more than I am always a pleasure to myself—but as my own being—so, don't talk or our separation again—it is impracticable. . . . (74)

Cathy's speech expressing her love for her father has a simple, logical structure. She begins with a brief statement of her feeling, followed by a paraphrase of the first sentence. She then continues with a statement of the logical effect of her feelings, then returns to the expression of her feeling of love with an amplification and proof. Finally, she repeats the amplified version of her expression. She maintains the unity of the speech by her repetition of the subject I and simple conjunction and.

Although Cathy's statement is persuasive, an attempt to convince Nelly of her love for her father, Catherine's is an assertion of truth. The structure of Catherine's speech is climactic, but it lacks the logical unity and cohesion Cathy's shows. The speech begins in confusion—she cannot express the certainty she feels, but feels it nonetheless and assumes others feel it as well. The embedding and interruption in the first sentence express her struggle to find the right words. The remainder of the speech presents the conclusion that Heathcliff is an extension of Catherine's self, which he always has been and always will be, regardless of circumstances. She concludes finally that kind of love is different from the type she feels for Edger Linton. The statements are not proof but rather assertions of truth. Her speech is thus a statement of conviction rather than of persuasion.

Because Cathy's love is active, the verbs she uses such as fret, care, do, say, love, know, and pray are dynamic, with most implying an act of volition. Her expression of love consequently can be seen as a statement of will. In contrast, Catherine expresses her love as a statement of being, and her verbs are stative. Cathy frets about her father's illness, but Catherine's miseries "have been" Heathcliff's. Cathy cares for nothing in comparison to her father, but Catherine's thought in living "is" Heathcliff. Unlike her daughter's verbs of action, Catherine's verbs throughout the speech express her metaphysical certainty. If Heathcliff existed, though all else perished,

Catherine knows she would continue to be; likewise, if he were annihilated, she is certain she would be alienated from the universe. Unlike the tone of understatement and simplicity Cathy's speech expresses, Catherine's derives energy from the resonance of the emphatic statements of being, combined with the amplifying modifiers in the predicate.

In addition to the contrast in verbs, the speeches differ in their substantives. Cathy expresses her love as a personal statement— each sentence begins with the subject I. Further, her substantives are concrete, of the "real world." She concerns herself with her father, his illness, and how her words might affect him. Catherine, conversely, expresses her love as a universal truth. She asserts, "There is or should be an existence of yours beyond you" (74). Her substantives are abstract, in the end metaphorical.

The third set of parallel speeches occurs when each character finds herself in isolation. After the fight between Heathcliff and Edgar, Catherine locks herself in her chamber where she grieves herself into madness. Echoing yet parodying her mother's self-imposed isolation, Cathy is tricked into entering Wuthering Heights, then captured and trapped in Linton's chamber where she grieves nearly to madness. Before her period of isolation, each character petitions for assistance. Catherine tells Nelly how distraught she is:

> I'm nearly distracted, Nelly! . . . A thousand smiths' hammers are beating in my head! Tell Isabella to shun me—this uproar is owing to her; and should she or anyone else aggravate my anger at present, I shall get wild, And, Nelly, say to Edgar, if you see him again to-night, that I'm in danger of being seriously ill. I wish it may prove true. He has startled and distressed me shockingly! I want to frighten him. Besides, he might come and begin a string of abuse, or complainings; I'm certain I should recriminate, and God knows where we should end! Will you do so, my good Nelly? You are aware that I am no way blameable in this matter. What possessed him to turn listener? Heathcliff's talk was outrageous, after you left us; but I could soon have diverted him from Isabella, and the rest meant nothing. Now, all is dashed wrong by the fool's craving to hear evil of self that haunts some people like demon! Had Edgar never gathered our conversation, he would have been the worse for it. Really, when he opened on me in that unreasonable tone of displeasure, after I had scolded Heathcliff till I was hoarse for *him*, I did not care, hardly, what they did to each other, especially as I felt that, however the scene closed, we should all be driven asunder for nobody knows how long! Well, if I cannot keep Heathcliff for my friend, if Edgar will be mean and jealous, I'll try to break their hearts by breaking my own. That will be a prompt way of finishing all, when I am pushed to extremity! But

it's a deed to be reserved for a forlorn hope; I'll not take Linton by surprise with it. To this point he has been discreet in dreading to provoke me; you must represent the peril of quitting that policy, and remind him of my passionate temper, verging, when kindled, on frenzy. I wish you could dismiss that apathy, out of your countenance, and look rather more anxious about me! (100–101)

Cathy promises Heathcliff that she will marry Linton if he will only allow her to return to Thrushcross Grange:

I'll not retract my word. . . . I'll marry him, within this hour, if I may go to Thrushcross Grange afterwards. Mr. Heathcliff, you're a cruel man, but you're not a fiend; and you won't, from *mere* malice, destroy irrevocably, all my happiness. If papa thought I had left him on purpose, and if he died before I returned, could I bear to live? I've given over crying; but I'm going to kneel her, at your knee; and I'll not get up, and I'll not take my eyes from your face, till you look back at me! No, don't turn away! *Do* look! You'll see nothing to provoke you. I don't hate you. I'm not angry that you struck me. Have you never loved *anybody*, in all your life, uncle? *Never*? Ah! you must look once—I'm so wretched—you can't help being sorry and pitying me. (219)

In addition to the obvious difference in length, the language of the two speeches demonstrates the contrast in principles. Catherine's words are more vivid, her verbs and adjectives more forceful than Cathy's. When she is the subject, however, her verbs are stative and, when she is object, they are dynamic—suggesting a strange sort of passivity. She says, for example, that she is not blamable for the occurrence that day, that Edgar startled and distressed her. The intensity results from the combination of dynamic actions of others and the participles expressing her condition or the condition of her world. She is "nearly distracted" and "pushed to extremity"; they all certainly will "be driven asunder"; "all is dashed wrong." Catherine rages and rails but does not act except in a self-destructive way—she will break her own heart if pushed to that extreme position. Catherine rarely uses the future tense other than with the subjunctive, asserting the ways things will inevitably turn out but taking little part in moving the action.

Cathy's words, though less vivid, attempt to persuade. Most of her verbs are active and dynamic—when she is the subject as well as when she mentions the actions of her father or uncle. It is only when she expresses her perceptions or describes her status that she uses stative verbs. At the end of her petition, for example, she assures Heathcliff that she is not angry, then attempts to persuade him to pity her because she is so wretched. Not only are her verbs generally dynamic, but they are expressions of her willingness to act. Cathy insists that she will marry Linton if Heathcliff will allow her to go home, and will not move from her position of supplication or take her eyes from him until he faces her. Indeed, in contrast to her mother's avoidance of the future tense, Cathy's repeated choice of future tense demonstrates her faith in her own ability to take action.

Thus, the two speeches can be seen to contrast a character who recognizes that she is controlled by forces beyond her will with one who attempts to persuade. Although Catherine's petition to Nelly attempts to compel her to act through an appeal to the authority of truth, Cathy's petition to Heathcliff attempts to compel him through what she considers shared assumptions. Neither speech achieves its objectives, however, because Nelly does not share Catherine's vision of truth, nor does Heathcliff share Cathy's definition of reasonable behavior. Thus, we might conclude that Emily Brontë does not contrast the two principles in any attempt to demonstrate that one is morally superior to the other, but rather to show that they are different and irreconcilable. Each view, with both limitations and strengths, is appropriate to the character who espouses it, but neither is completely efficacious.

Unlike Malory (who uses role to differentiate characters of the same type) and Sidney (who contrasts different philosophical types), Emily Brontë contrasts characters who appear to be inherently the same psychological type yet turn out to be quite different both philosophically and psychologically. Indeed, Emily Brontë contrasts not only the worlds of Wuthering Heights and Thrushcross Grange but also two parallel but quite different world views. Each principle is presented through a character whose individuation and type are expressed partly through her dialogue. Although maintaining their general similarities in type, Brontë assigns each character idiosyncratic, individual linguistic patterns—dictional, syntactic, and rhetorical—uniquely appropriate both to her world and idea of the self. Mother and daughter are both naturally passionate and intense; yet Catherine, raised in the atmosphere of Wuthering Heights, exemplifies full-blown passion, whereas Cathy, raised in Thrushcross Grange, represents softened passion. Both are naturally impetuous and somewhat selfish; yet coming from and representing a world of nature in which events have their own logic, Catherine sees the world determined by forces that are beyond the understanding of human logic. Because Cathy, however, is born in and stands for a civilized world in which actions have logical consequences, she thus has faith in the power of persuasion.

The overwhelming response of most readers to *Wuthering Heights*, however, has always been intensely connected to the speeches of Catherine. The line remembered most frequently from Brontë's work is Catherine's passionate declaration "I am Heathcliff" (74). One reason we leave *Wuthering Heights* recalling Catherine's words and somehow forgetting those of her daughter is because of their poetic resonance. Beyond poetry, however, Catherine's words seem to ring true in Emily Brontë's world. For all her passionate railing against the controlling forces, Catherine recognizes truths about herself and the world she inhabits, and when she can no longer live within that world, she departs. In contrast, Cathy molds herself to fit the world. Rather than persuading the people around her to recreate themselves according to her desires, she fulfills the role for which she was raised. Once she has polished Hareton's rough edges, she will take her rightful place as the lady of Thrushcross Grange. Despite her early adventures, she will return to the confines of the garden wall. Thus, both characters illustrate what appears to be a central truth in the world of *Wuthering Heights*— that individuals do not control their destinies but are instead carved out of their environments. Despite their most valiant efforts, they cannot make the world fulfill their desires.[21]

Thus, in one sense, the work is indeed a psychological case study to the extent that it explores the effect of environment on an individual, and yet it is also a metaphysical romance with characters who represent visions of truth. The two modes fuse artistically; as Walter Allen has noted, Catherine and Cathy "convince because they so completely express in themselves and their behavior the laws of their being, which are their creator's deductions—artistic deductions—from the findings of her intuition into the nature of things."[22]

5
Conclusions

This study began by questioning the critical practices based on the traditional assumption that romance is a highly conventional genre. Having recognized its conventionality, critics of romance rarely examine the genre closely for subtleties of technique, but all too often focus on only the idea that the work illustrates and its conventions, not on the rhetoric of those conventions. Considerations of the text recede before those of meaning and allegory. Northrop Frye, noting this lack of critical attention to technique, has argued that romances in many ways resemble abstract paintings and, like modern art, require a sensitivity on the part of the literary critic to the ways they differ from more representational art forms. The figures in the great abstract paintings of the twentieth-century are conventional; yet critics of modern art would never deny and consequently ignore the artist's skill in creating such abstractions. Although the conventions of romance differ from those of abstract paintings, it is no less important to examine closely the techniques or romance—an examination I have attempted with regard to one specific technique: the definition of characters through dialogue.

Critics of fiction accept the notion that authors define characters, at least in part, by the words they speak. Although many works on fiction mention the technique of establishing character through dialogue, few address the technique directly or discuss a methodology for its examination. Robie Macauley and George Lanning, in their *Technique in Fiction*, specifically address authorial methods of establishing character through discourse. In their examination of speech in fiction, they assert that "one of the most important purposes of speech is to express character."[1] Discussing the options available to the writer, they explain that the writer "must vary his rhythms, his vocabulary, the length or brevity of a speech as much as he can and make them conform as closely as possible to what would be true of the particular character."[2] They continue later, "a fundamental rule of fiction that is worth emphasizing several times is that each character should express his personality in what he says: in its rhythms, locutions, idiosyncracies, brevity or longwindedness, and syntactic structure."[3]

As Macauley and Lanning indicate, a study of the technique of defining characters through dialogue requires some application of textual criticism, stylistics, or rhetorical analysis. An application of such methodologies reveals subtleties of language writers use to define their characters. This study suggests that such a methodology may be employed to examine techniques of romance characterization as well, an observation accepted by several medieval scholars who have noted the way writers of romance define character types through their manners of speaking. None of the discussions of voice in romance, however, considers the ways conventions of speech have been used to show differences. Subtleties of expression may not only represent types but also differentiate characters of the same type according to the rhetorical situation.

The works of Thomas Malory, Philip Sidney, and Emily Brontë illustrate three different ways conventions of dialogue may be used to develop and contrast parallel typed characters according to the demands of the work. All three writers distinguish between characters of the same basic type through variations in dialogue. Of the three works, the *Morte Darthur* relies most heavily on abstract conventions by employing repeated patterns of formula and structure of speech. In addition, Malory's world represents a very narrowly defined social class. The limited number of social types joined with the conventionality of the language results in characters who exhibit more similarities than differences in dialogue. As the same type, Guinevere and Isode often use the same syntax, formula, or formal structure of their speeches. The two queens differ, however, in their relationships with other characters and thus in the roles they play in the romance. Because the language is so conventional, Malory is able to mark shifts in relationships with even slight changes in form, and, in these contexts, modulations in voice reflect differences in the role the character plays in the plot. In one role, a marked difference in speaking styles separates the two queens. In their roles as lovers, Isode's style of discourse remains constant regardless of context, whereas Guinevere's style varies, becoming more formal when she addresses Lancelot in public and less so in private. Because their styles are similar elsewhere, the contrast draws attention to Guinevere's fluctuations. Further, because Malory explicitly underlines Guinevere's association with the Round Table, her inconsistency can be seen rhetorically to illustrate Malory's view of the weakness in the fellowship of the Round Table.

In the *New Arcadia*, Sidney also uses conventions to illustrate the similarity in characters when they represent the same type and disparity when their roles differ. He uses the same character, however, to represent philosophical as well as societal types. Although Pamela and Philoclea speak similarly when they represent princesses, they speak quite differently when they represent the contrasting philosophical types of Majesty and Beauty. Like Malory, Sidney contrasts roles the characters play by placing them in particular narrative contexts that demand different conventions of speech. He also delineates differences between the characters as philosophical ideas by distinguishing between their manners of speaking in similar narrative contexts. Sidney's technique of characterization differs from Malory's in the kinds of speech conventions he employs. Rather than using conventions of formula, Sidney varies his characters' rhetorical tropes and figures.

Emily Brontë's technique of characterization reveals a concept of character that differs from those of Malory or Sidney. Unlike the queens in *Le Morte* or the two queens in the *Arcadia*, Catherine Earnshaw Linton and her daughter Cathy Linton display relatively stable, idiosyncratic speech patterns. Although conventions differentiate the two voices, context often intensifies these patterns but never varies them significantly. The individuation of characters shows them as having perhaps the most fully developed mimetic attributes, whereas their thematic functions seem to dominate any mimetic function; the attributes coalesce to present principles, or abstract symbols, of two very different and incompatible world views.

Thus, the findings of this study suggest that although characters in romance are conventional, predictable, often static, and, to varying degrees, abstract, they can also be complex and richly detailed. The writers of *Le Morte Darthur*, the *New Arcadia*, and *Wuthering Heights* employ techniques of characterization parallel to those of more mimetic fiction. Like the writers of realism, these writers apply the notion that "style is the man" to what Stephen Ullmann has identified as "the need to portray a character through his speech."[4] P. M. Wetherill has observed that one of the findings of critics using stylistic analyses has been that a character in fiction may be expressed through grammar as well as by moral attitudes or even by a combination of the two.[5] Wetherill's observation applies to the characters of romance as well as mimetic character. A close reading of parallel characters' speech conventions reveals that romance characters, like realistic characters, can indeed be expressed by their manner of speaking. Regardless of the types of conventions em-

ployed, regardless of the genre, the author creates fictional characters, at least in part by the speeches assigned to that character.

Because parallel romance characters tend to use the same conventions, often the same words, critics have overlooked subtle differences in characters of the same type. Such differences, however,
are important to the complexity of the composition. In romance,
perhaps even more than in more representational fiction, seeing the
entire composition is essential for a sensitive reading because, like
the abstract painting, a romance presents an ideal or an idealized
montage in a static form. In the three romances considered here, the
writers have created patterns of meaning through fine distinctions
of word choice, rhetorical conventions, syntax, and the structure of
speeches. The discovery of such complexity suggests that writers of
romances may use sophisticated techniques of composition similar
in means to those employed by writers of mimetic fiction. Like the
abstract painter who creates art with the same materials as the painter of realism, the writer of romance works within the same conventions of grammar and rhetoric, of character and plot. One variation,
however, that Norman Friedman has observed is that "found in a
difference of end and consequently in how this end causes the organization of the whole to look and feel somewhat different."[6]

While employing techniques of characterization similar to those
of the writers of mimetic fiction, writers of romance may subtly
differentiate characters to illustrate patterns of meaning at the philosophical centers of their works. These patterns are created by conventions of language and thus represent not personalities but ideas,
world views, models of decorum. Such a suggestion is perhaps what
Edwin Muir had in mind when he argued that flat characters can
have a complexity as rich as but different from that of round
characters.[7] Seen as patterns of meaning, romance characters illustrate the contention of Wellek and Warren that romance deals with
a deeper psychology than does realistic fiction.[8]

This study raises several related issues that are beyond the limits
of its controlling question. First, it would be interesting to discover
whether other writers of what have been considered more conventional romances differentiate characters of the same type, or
whether Malory, Sidney, and Brontë, writing sophisticated forms
of the romance, rise above the limitations of their form. Further,
it remains to be discovered whether writers of Middle English,
English Renaissance, and nineteenth-century Gothic romances
employed speech conventions unique to their particular genre, and
whether a grammar of romance traditions existed. Stylistic analysis
could help define the rhetoric of dialogue in each of the romance

traditions, with the language of the paticular text examined in light of the ways it differs from or echoes related works from the same period.

The study of character in fiction, including the use and techniques of development, is still a largely unexplored area. Recent studies have raised important questions concerning the function of characters, their relationship to plot and idea, their functions in the text, and even what constitutes character. The use of characters in romance seems an ever-intriguing area of study because so many a priori assumptions concerning romance characters have been accepted for so long. Although certainly not providing a definitive explanation of techniques of romance characterization, this study questions old premises and attempts to show how an examination of character, which is not bound by such restrictive assumptions, can provide new perspectives on the text. Thus, this work suggests that formal stylistic, or rhetorical analysis, of character can help establish a unifying principle, a pattern that may well prove to illuminate the complexity of the whole.

Notes

Preface

1. Northrop Frye, *The Secular Scripture: A Study of the Structure of Romance* (Cambridge: Harvard University Press, 1976), 38.

Chapter 1. Characterization in Romance

1. Michael Davitt Bell, *The Development of American Romance: The Sacrifice of Relation* (Chicago: University of Chicago Press, 1980), 7–22. For Reeves definition of romance, see René Wellek and Austin Warren's *Theory of Literature* (New York: Harcourt, Brace, 1949), 216. Like Bell, Frederic Jameson distinguishes between two major definitions of the genre: the semantic and the syntactic approaches; according to the first, romance is defined thematically, according to the second, formally ("Magical Narratives: Romance as Genre," *NLH* 7 [1975]: 35–163).

2. See the definition of romance found in Wellek and Warren's *Theory of Literature*, 216. Romance, they observe "may neglect verisimilitude of detail (the reproduction of individuated speech in dialogue, for example), addressing itself to a higher reality, a deeper psychology."

3. W. P. Ker, *Epic and Romance* (1896; reprint, London: Macmillan,1922), 368.

4. Most modern critics attribute the conventional nature of romance characters to the author's interest in abstract ideas. Unlike novels, which are generally understood to be concerned with revealing and exploring character, romances are said to contain conventional or abstract characters created to represent abstract ideals or ideas. Of representatives of this view, Northrop Frye's definition is perhaps the best known and most often quoted:

> The characterization of romance follows its general dialectic structure, which means that subtlety and complexity are not much favored. Characters tend to be either for or against the quest. If they assist it they are idealized as simply gallant or pure; if they obstruct it they are caricatured as simply villainous or cowardly. (*Anatomy of Criticism* [Princeton: Princeton University Press, 1957], 195)

Other critics who have written on romance generally begin with Frye's definition. Gillian Beer, for example, adds that because romances appeal to shared human desires, they portray idealizations—characters with a heroic quality that universalizes them (*Romance* [London: Methuen, 1970], 2–3). John Stevens identifies the writer's preoccupation with idealizing as the inspiration of all the romance's conventions (*Medieval Romance: Themes and Approaches* [London: Hutchinson University Library, 1973], 17).

5. Dorothy Van Ghent has observed such moments in *Pilgrim's Progress*, but finds the "homely accuracy of detail," although charming, to be somewhat distracting (*The English Novel: Form and Function* [New York: Rinehart, 1953], 22–23).

6. Nathaniel Hawthorne, *The House of Seven Gables* (New York: Washington Square Press, 1970).

7. Hawthorne's masterpiece has been seen variously as, for example, an exploration of the role of the artist in society (Joel Porte, *The Romance in America: Studies in Cooper, Poe, Hawthorne, Melville and James* [Middletown, Conn.: Wesleyan University Press, 1969]), a study of isolation (John C. Gerber, "Form and Content in *The Scarlet Letter*," *New England Quarterly* 17 [1944]: 26–28, 29–34), of guilt (Frederick C. Crews, *The Sins of the Fathers* [London: Oxford University Press, 1966]), or of revenge (Mark Van Doren, *Nathaniel Hawthorne* [New York: William Sloane, 1949]).

8. See Leland Schubert's *Hawthorne, the Artist* (Chapel Hill: The University of North Carolina Press, 1944) and Gordon Roper's introduction to *The Scarlet Letter and Selected Prose Works* (New York: Farrar, Straus, 1949). Matthiessen discusses the structure of *The Scarlet Letter* in his *American Renaissance: Art and Expression in the Age of Emerson and Whitman* (London: Oxford University Press, 1941), 275–82.

9. Dolis uses the term specifically in reference to Pearl's reflection in the water as illustrative of her shadowy wrath ("Hawthorne's Metonymic Gaze: Image and Object," *American Literature* 56 [1984]: 369–70).

10. For an interesting discussion of Spenser's choice of conventions to illustrate his idea, see Susanne Lindgren Wofford's "Britomart's Petrachan Lament: Allegory and Narrative in *The Fairie Queene* III, iv," *Comparative Literature* 39 (1987): 28–57, in which she shows Spenser using Petrarchan laments to create a particular allusive context.

11. Hochman generally objects to the structuralist and poststructuralist views of characters as construct. Acknowledging his debt to Virginia Woolf, as well as to William J. Harvey, Hochman argues that the reader sees characters in fictional works in much the same ways as people in life—first as types, or in terms of generalizations about types, then as unique individuals. What Hochman objects to in works such as Chatman's *Story and Discourse: Narrative Structure in Fiction and Film.* (Ithaca: Cornell University Press, 1978) or Richard Lanham's *Motives of Eloquence: Literary Rhetoric in the Renaissance* (New Haven: Yale University Press, 1976). is their view of all characters as static patterns (*Character in Literature* [Ithaca: Cornell University Press, 1985], 77).

12. Frye, *Secular Scripture*, 53.

13. Frye, *Anatomy of Criticism*, 305.

14. Since works of Frye and Auerbach (*Mimesis: The Representation of Reality in Western Literature*, trans. Willard R. Trask [Princeton: Princeton University Press] 1953), published in the 1950s, the lines between critical approaches to character have been distinctly drawn. Seymour Chatman explains the typical distinction made by contemporary critics when he notes that most maintain the Aristotelian contrast between agent (*pratton*) and character (*ethos*). Agents are defined by the action, with their traits always "provocative of action," but characters are added on, their traits being psychological rather than dependent upon function (*Story and Discourse*, 108–10). Most formalist and structuralist theories, such as those of Propp, Todorov, Greimas, and Culler, analyze characters functionally—as partici-

pants; although they may recognize the existence of the second category, they avoid any consideration of the psychological essence of character. In one of the most recent studies of character, Thomas Docherty also questions the mimetic assumption and offers a postmodernist reading of character that examines the interaction of the writer's language and the reader (*Reading [Absent] Character: Towards a Theory of Characterization in Fiction* [Oxford: Clarendon Press, 1983]). Theories of character as ethos can be found in three major works written since the mid-1960s: William J. Harvey's *Character and the Novel* (Ithaca: Cornell University Press, 1965), Martin Price's *Forms of Life: Character and Moral Imagination in the Novel* (New Haven: Yale University Press, 1983), and Baruch Hochman's *Character in Literature.* All three critics operate on the assumption that fiction creates the illusion of a lived experience through its characters, though certainly to varying degrees. For a recent survey of various approaches to the study of character, see John Frow's "Spectacle Binding: On Character," *Poetics Today* 7 (1986): 227–50.

15. The critical neglect of romance characterization may be due, at least in part, to the tendency of twentieth-century criticism to evaluate romance characters in terms of mimetic fiction. In fact, the early twentieth-century studies of fiction singled out a new use of character as one of the chief identifying features of the novel form. Ernest A. Baker's *The History of the English Novel* (London: H. F. and G. Wetherby, 1924), 1:11, for example, defined the novel specifically in terms of its use of characters, and found the new form different from and by implication better than romance, which "had little to do with ordinary life." A more explicit judgment of romance character was presented by E. M. Forster, in his *Aspects of the Novel* (New York: Harcourt, Brace, 1927); he viewed romances as less interesting than novels because of romance's neglect of reality and its use of conventional or abstract characters (103–25).

There were dissenters from this derision of the typed character, however, even as early as the 1920s. Edwin Muir, for example, in his *The Study of the Novel* (London: Hogarth, 1928), 146, attempts to rescue typed characters from critical scorn, and, in doing so, implies the need for greater attention to romance characterization. He argues that such characters, though typical, may have a spatial vitality expressed by a formula or a number of formulas. Thus, he concludes, the complexity of a typed character is not less true but only different from that of a round character. In addition to Muir, other critics later exhibited similar sentiments and evaluated characters according to their function in the narrative structure rather than for their neglect of reality. René Wellek and Austin Warren, for example, argue that romance addresses itself to "a higher reality, a deeper psychology" (*Theory of Literature*, 224).

Certainly, the differences between antirepresentational and realistic ought to be explored, but presently the old terminology continues to color the interpretation of characters in romance. An interesting discussion of the distinctions can be found in James Phelan's analysis of the critical debate; see "Character, Progression, and the Mimetic-Didactic Distinction," *Modern Philology* 84 (1978): 282–99. As Phelan explains, critics tend to view characters as possible persons, as carriers of ideas, or as artificial constructs. Phelan proposes a less rigid delineation. Examining the nature of characters in their respective narratives, he distinguishes a character's dimensions from its function. All characters, Phelan explains, have attributes or traits. As dimensions, these attributes may work to show the character as a possible person, a representative of a class or a carrier of ideas, as well as a participant in the structure of the text. This dimension, however, is typically subsumed into the function that character is fulfilling in the narrative—mimetic, thematic, or structural.

16. Chatman, *Story and Discourse*, 132.

17. Marie Borroff, trans. *Sir Gawain and the Green Knight: A New Verse Translation* (New York: W.W. Norton, 1967).

18. See John Stevens's discussion of Gawain's style of discourse as an example of thematic unity in medieval romance (*Medieval Romance*, 172–74). Two other recent works shed light on the rhetorical use of character: Patricia A. Parker's *Inescapable Romance: Studies in the Poetics of a Mode* (Princeton: Princeton University Press, 1979) and Warren Ginsberg's *The Cast of Character: The Representation of Pesonality in Ancient and Medieval Literature* (Toronto: University of Toronto Press, 1983). In a discussion of Eve in *Paradise Lost*, Parker argues that Eve's moment of self-reflection as she gazes on her image in the smooth lake becomes an emblem of all suspensions within Milton's epic. Similarly, Ginsberg demonstrates that medieval writers employed principles of typology as a feature of narrative structure, and that frequently characters introduced early in a text prefigure later characters, themes, and structures—thus establishing a typological pattern of foreshadowing and fulfillment. As an example of this technique, Ginsberg points to Chretien's *Yvain* in which the early adventure of one of Arthur's knights both prefigures Yvain's later exploits and implies the entire Arthurian story.

19. P. M. Wetherill, for example, has observed in *The Literary Text: An Examination of Critical Methods* (Berkeley: University of California Press, 1974), 36–71, that one of the findings of critics using stylistic analyses has been that character in fiction may be expressed through grammar as well as by moral attitudes. See also Baruch Hochman's discussion of the ways writers of fiction establish and distinguish between characters through the words they speak (*Character in Literature*, 72–76). For earlier discussions of the relationship between character and style, see Dorothy Van Ghent's *The English Novel: Form and Function* (New York: Rínehart, 1953) and Walter Allen's *The English Novel: A Short Critical History* (New York: E. P. Dutton, 1954), as well as Erich Auerbach's *Mimesis* and Northrop Frye's *Anatomy of Criticism*.

20. In the 1950s, the works of Dorothy Van Ghent (*The English Novel*), Walter Allen (*The English Novel*), as well as Erich Auerbach (*Mimesis*) and Northrop Frye (*Anatomy of Criticism*), echoed Mark Schorer's earlier contention that language is part of the technique of fiction ("Fiction and the 'Analogical Matrix,'" *Kenyon Review* 11 [Autumn 1949]; reprinted in *Critiques and Essays on Modern Fiction 1920–1951*, ed. John W. Aldridge. [New York: Ronald, 1952], 83–98), by applying the study of prose style to a consideration of character. Van Ghent considers diction and syntax to be the ways writers create individual characters. She observes, for example, that Bunyan establishes his characters by "the precise and inevitable tone of voice, the mood of the verb, and idiom, and the syntactic rhythm." Walter Allen also notes Bunyan's vivid characterization and natural dialogue as well as Henry Fielding's and Jane Austen's dramatic methods of presenting action through a succession of short scenes in dialogue, with the words the characters speak establishing their character traits. Auerbach's study was a landmark because it not only affected the ways critics have considered character, but it also was the first to explore to a significant degree the relationship between character and style. Finally, Northrop Frye specifically mentions style of direct discourse as a technique of character definition:

> Dialogue has to speak with the voice of the internal characters, not the author, and sometimes dialogue and narrative are so far apart as to divide the book into different languages. The suiting of style to an internal character or subject is known as decorum or appropriateness of style to content. Decorum is in general the poet's *ethical* voice, the modification of his own voice to the voice of a character or to the vocal tone demanded by subject or mood.

21. Charles Muscatine, *Chaucer and the French Tradition* (Berkeley: University of California Press, 1964), 184.

22. Cecily Clark, "*Sir Gawain and the Green Knight*: Characterization by Syntax," *Essays in Criticism* 16 (1966): 361–74.

23. P. J. C. Field, *Romance and Chronicle: A Study of Malory's Prose Style* (Bloomington: Indiana University Press, 1971), 129.

24. See especially chapter 7, "The Wordes Moote be Cosyn to the Dede" (*Chaucer's English* [London: Andre Deutsch, 1974], 370), where he argues that:

> Chaucer is keenly aware of the way different people speak and there are many indications that he is creating differentiations or, if we so prefer, different registers, for his various characters. This does not mean closely sustained verisimilitude of tone and diction according to any strictly naturalistic canons, but rather a more general labelling of a person's speech which affords the reader occasional moments of pleased recognition.

25. John E. Stevens, *Medieval Romance: Themes and Approaches* (London: Hutchinson University Library, 1973), 172–74.

26. Eugène Vinaver, ed., *The Works of Sir Thomas Malory*, 2nd ed. (London: Oxford University Press, 1967), 1128. Subsequent quotations from this work are cited parenthetically in the text.

27. Peter R. Schroeder, "Hidden Depths: Dialogue and Characterization in Chaucer and Malory," *Publications of the Modern Language Association* 98 (1983): 377.

28. Nathaniel Hawthorne, *The Scarlet Letter* (New York: New American Library, 1959), 175.

Chapter 2. Queenly Decorum in *Le Morte Darthur*

1. Muir, *Study of the Novel*, 3.

2. Mark Lambert, *Style and Vision in Le Morte Darthur* (New Haven: Yale University Press, 1975), 94.

3. Dhira B. Mahoney, "Narrative Treatment of Name in Malory's *Morte D'Arthur*," *ELH* 47 (1980): 655.

4. See, for example, the stylistic analyses of Field and Lambert, as well as comments by Brewer in the introduction to his modernization of *Le Morte Darthur* and Benson's discussion of Malory and Middle English romance in his study of Malory's work (P. J. C. Field, *Romance and Chronicle: A Study of Malory's Prose Style*. [Bloomington: Indiana University Press, 1971]; Lambert, *Style and Vision*, D. S. Brewer, *The Morte Darthur, Parts Seven and Eight by Sir Thomas Malory* [Evanston, Ill.: Northwestern University Press, 1968]; Larry D. Benson, *Malory's Morte Darthur* [Cambridge: Harvard University Press, 1976]).

5. Lambert, *Style and Vision*, 110–13.

6. Schroeder, "Chaucer and Malory," 375.

7. Stevens, *Medieval Romance*, See especially chapter 8, "Realism and Romance: Charaters and Types."

8. Stevens, 169.

9.

	Guinevere	Isode
Mean sentence length	18.7	20.5
Number of sentences per speech	1.8	1.7
Number of words per speech	30.9	35.36
Number of clauses per speech	2.5	2.9

10.

	Guinevere	Isode
Main clauses	1.277	1.419
Adjusted for different sentence length	.091	.089
Percentage of		
Adjectives	5%	4.3%
Nouns	13%	13.6%
Verbs	17.5%	16.5%

11.

	Guinevere	Isode
Percentage of sentences		
Beginning with coordinate conjunctions	34.5%	19%
Beginning with a subject	10%	11%
Beginning with a vocative	19%	19%
Beginning with an interjection or adverbial disjunct (e.g., certainly, well, truly)	13.9%	11%
Beginning with a verb	9.5%	4.8%

12. Sentence components in seven different narrative contexts:

	Sentence Length	Main Clauses	Dep. Clauses	Phrases	Nouns	Verbs.	Pros.	Adjs.	Advs.
1. Private conversations with Lancelot or Tristram									
Guinevere	22.4	1.5	1.4	1.95	3.3	3.5	4.6	.9	1.6
Isode	22.5	1.5	1.6	2	3	3.5	4	.9	.9
2. Public conversations with Lancelot or Tristram									
Guinevere	16	1.3	1.2	1.3	1.8	2.8	3.3	.6	1.2
Isode	23.9	1.4	1.8	1.8	3.1	3.4	5.4	1.3	1.8
3. Conversations with captors									
Guinevere	15.3	1.2	1.2	.8	1.6	2.7	3.5	.8	.9
Isode	18.6	1.4	2	1.4	1.8	3.6	5.6	.8	.8
4. Conversations with knights									
Guinevere	18.5	1.2	1.3	1.7	3	2.8	3.3	1.1	.8
Isode	21.1	1.5	1.6	1.9	3.2	3.2	3.5	.9	.8
5. Conversations with King Arthur or King Mark									
Guinevere	12.1	1.1	.5	1.5	1.4	2.5	2.8	.4	.6
Isode	8.8	1.5	.5	.5	1.3	2	2.3	.3	.3

13. P. J. C. Field, *Romance and Chronicle: A Study of Malory's Prose Style* (Bloomington: Indiana University Press, 1971), 115.

14. D. S. Brewer, commenting on this passage, remarks that "how moving is that brief change to the warmth and intimacy of the second person singular." Brewer thinks that Malory achieves a delicate effect here with minimal means (*Morte Darthur*, 15).

15. This passage is, in fact, one example Schroeder points to as an example of Guinevere's non sequiturs ("Chaucer and Malory," 374–87).

16. Charles Moorman, *The Book of Kyng Arthur: The Unity of Malory's Morte Darthur* (Lexington: University of Kentucky Press, 1965), 25.

17. Chatman, *Story and Discourse*, 132.

18. Benson, *Malory's Morte Darthur*, 79.

19. Field, *Romance and Chronicle*, 107–19.
20. Lambert, *Style and Vision*, 45, 109–13.
21. Ibid., 117.
22. In his comments on the passage that includes the code, Eugène Vinaver notes that the code is Malory's invention. "This is perhaps the most complete and authentic record of Malory's conception of chivalry" (*Works of Malory*, 1335); whether Malory, however, found the code and the fellowship that was established to uphold it exemplary is another issue. Thomas Wright sees shortcomings in the code itself. It is, he argues, "too inflexible and too static; it cannot embrace enough of the contingencies in the human situation. Indeed, though it may at first inspire order and impose justice it becomes finally the weakest aspect of Camelot because the Arthurian demonology which it expresses is weak ("The Tale of King Arthur: Beginnings and Foreshadowings," in *Malory's Originality: A Critical Study of Le Morte Darthur*, ed. R. M. Lumiansky [Baltimore: Johns Hopkins, 1964], 32). In a somewhat different evaluation, Wilfred Guerin contends that by showing Arthur "trying to fashion a society which would uphold the Christian ethic," Malory assigns the tragedy to inevitable failure in "trying to bring paradise down to earth" ("The Tale of the Death of Arthur," in *Malory's Originality*, 273–74). Guerin concludes that Malory contrasts this tragedy with the only true way to achieve salvation—as an individual. Similarly, Moorman sees the chivalric system possessing the faults of internal dissention and inherent instability (*The Book of Kyng Arthur: The Unity of Malory's Morte Darthur* [Lexington: University of Kentucky Press, 1965], 47). In contrast, Edmund Reiss notes that the chivalric code was established at Pentecost, the feast celebrating "the descent to the world of the Holy Spirit, an act enabling the new order—represented by the Church—to come about." He argues, "The world of the Round Table is not in itself bad" rather, that for a few, courtliness "was the way to holiness." See *Sir Thomas Malory* (New York: Twayne, 1966), 38, 159, 191. Despite the differing views of the code, though, most readers of *Le Morte* agree that the fellowship became characterized by internal dissention and instability, and, as a result, fell.
23. Vinaver, *Works of Malory*, 1527.

Chapter 3. Platonic Ideas in the *New Arcadia*

1. See, for example, Lorna Challis, "The Use of Oratory in Sidney's *Arcadia*," *Studies in Philology* 62 (1965): 561–76; John Danby, *Poets on Fortune's Hill* (1952; reprinted as *Elizabethan and Jacobean Poets: Studies in Sidney, Shakespeare, Beaumont and Fletcher* [London: Faber and Faber, 1965]); P. Albert Duhamel, "Sidney's *Arcadia* and Elizabethan Rhetoric," *Studies in Philology* 62 (1965): 561–760; Richard A. Lanham, "The Old Arcadia," in *Sidney's Arcadia*, ed. Walter R. Davis and Richard A. Lanham (New Haven: Yale University Press, 1965); Kenneth O. Myrick, *Sir Philip Sidney as Literary Craftsman*, 2nd ed. (Lincoln: University of Nebraska Press, 1965); Neil Rudenstine, *Sidney's Poetic Development* (Cambridge: Harvard University Press, 1967); R. W. Zandvoort, *Sidney's 'Arcadia,' A Comparison Between the Two Versions* (Amsterdam: Swets and Zeitlinger, 1929).
2. Arthur Amos, *Time, Space, and Value: The Narrative Structure of the New Arcadia* (London: Associated University Press, 1977), 40.
3. Thelma N. Greenfield, *The Eye of Judgment: Reading the New Arcadia* (Lewisburg, Pa.: Bucknell University Press, 1982), 94–95.

4. Walter R. Davis, *Idea and Act in Elizabethan Fiction* (Princeton: Princeton University Press, 1969), 48.

5. Davis, 31.

6. Ibid., 44.

7. Norman Friedman, *Form and Meaning in Fiction* (Athens: University of Georgia Press, 1975), 109.

8. Albert Feuillerat, ed., *The Prose Works of Sir Philip Sidney*, vol. 4 (1912; reprint, Cambridge: Cambridge University Press, 1962).

9. Fulke Greville, *Life of Sir Philip Sidney*, quoted in John Danby, *Elizabethan and Jacobean Poets*, 46.

10. Nancy Lindheim, *The Structures of Sidney's Arcadia* (Toronto: University of Toronto Press, 1982), 25–26.

11. Lindheim, 29.

12. Feuillerat, *Works of Sidney*, 1:20. Subsequent quotations from this work are cited parenthetically in the text.

13. Lindheim, *Sidney's Arcadia*, 29.

14. Amos, *New Arcadia*, 140.

15. Greenfield has shown the ways this passage "gives example of how psychological experience finds expression through rhetorical finish" (*New Arcadia*, 87).

16. Gerold argues that the character development is almost the same as in a novel, and that "because of his gift for creating human characters, Sidney deserves far more than Lyly to be called the forerunner of the British novelists who were to come" (G. H. Gerould, *The Patterns of English and American Fiction: A History* [New York: Russell and Russell, 1966], 27).

Chapter 4. The Conflict of World Views in *Wuthering Heights*

1. At least part of *Wuthering Heights*'s enigma comes from its dialectic structure, both in the contrast of the two houses and of the two generations. In attempting to discover Emily Brontë's purpoe in creating the parallels, some early critics follow Lord David Cecil's famous essay in which he discusses the work as a metaphysical conflict of opposing principles ("Emily Brontë and Wuthering Heights," in *Early Victorian Novelists* [London: Bobbs-Merrill, 1935]; reprinted in *Wuthering Heights: An Authoritative Text with Essays in Criticism*, ed. William M. Sale, Jr. [New York: Norton, 1963], 287–305). Most of these interpretations focus on the story of Catherine and Heathcliff and read the work as a contrast of opposing values, with the various characters falling into one camp or the other.

Strangely enough, although such readings concern the contrast between the two houses, they are rarely concerned with the second generation and thus fail to come to terms with half of the text. Denis Donaghue, for example, identifies the characters as functions or projections of absolute definitive forces. He discusses Heathcliff and Catherine as forms of energy, but never mentions Cathy, Linton, and Hareton ("The Other Emily," in *The Brontës: A Collection of Critical Essays*, ed. Ian Gregor [Englewood Cliffs,: N. J.: Prentice-Hall, 1970], 157–72). Even Dorothy Van Ghent, who has brilliantly diagrammed the structure of the book, focuses her attention mainly on the Catherine, Edgar, and Heathcliff story, discussing the story of the second generation only as a modified version of the original (*The English Novel: Form and Function* [New York: Rinehart, 1953]). Seemingly, she agrees with Richard Chase's evaluation of Hareton and Cathy as merely insignificant reproductions of the first generation ("The Brontës, or Myth Domesticated," *Forms of Modern Fiction: Essays Collected in Honor of Joseph Warren Beach*, ed. William Van O'Connor. [Minneapolis: University of Minnesota Press, 1948], 102–19). In a recent interpretation, Sandra Gilbert and Susan Gubar find Catherine to be Brontë's focus; Cathy, though her mother's "non-identical double," is only one of many characters whose lives parallel Catherine's (*The Madwoman in the Attic: The Woman Writer and the Nineteenth-Century Literary Imagination* [New Haven: Yale University Press, 1979], 249–308).

The issue has also been approched from a sociological perspective, with the characters as types, though now as representatives of class rather than of forces or principles. These readings give rather more attention to Brontë's second generation and tend to see it in a somewhat more positive light than do the metaphysical readings. Arnold Kettle, for example, finds the love story of Cathy and Hareton as a vindication of the Catherine and Heathcliff story (*An Introduction to the English Novel*, vol. 1 [London: Hutchinson's University Library, 1951]); Q. D. Leavis argues that Cathy rights her mother's wrongs by freely choosing Hareton ("A Fresh Approach to Wuthering Heights," *Lectures in America*, ed. F. R. Leavis and Q. D. Leavis [New York: Random House, 1969]), 83–149; and Terry Eagleton, although reading the ending as essentially tragic, believes it symbolically proposes a future that "lies with a fusion rather than a confrontation of interests between gentry and bourgeoisie" (*Myths of Power: A Marxist Study of the Brontës* [London: Macmillan, 1975], 116).

Of the various approaches to the dilemma, the one most interested in Brontë's characterization has been those readings that see *Wuthering Heights* as a psychological case study. Adherents to this position tend to see more subtlety of characterization than either the metaphysical or sociological readers, and few of these readers dismiss the second generation as insignificant. Muriel Spark and Derek Stanford, for example, argue that we do not view either Catherine or Cathy in terms of recurrent gesture or phrase" (*Emily Brontë: Her Life and Work* [New York: Coward-McCann, 1966], 246). Indeed, Colin Wilson calls Catherine almost an archetypal female outsider type but says nothing of her daughter ("A Personal Response to *Wuthering Heights*," in *The Art of Emily Brontë*, ed. Ann Smith [London: Vision, 1976], 236), and Leo Bersani sees little difference in the development of the two characters (except in finding the second half of the book merely "a cute story of how antagonism changes to love," thus denying the vision of the Catherine and Heathcliff section, *A Future for Astyanax: Character and Desire in Literature* [Boston: Little, Brown, 1969], 222). Most of the critics, however, who examine the psychology of the characters see Cathy as an interesting character, or at least worthy of discussion, whether she is viewed as emotionally a more mature woman or psychologically a healthier woman or merely a conventionalized replay of her mother.

In contrast to Bersani's view, John E. Jordan has argued that although Cathy's love may be a kind of maternal perversion, Catherine's is a selfish passion, and consequently we are asked to see Cathy both as a weak echo and a finer human being ("The Ironic Vision of Emily Brontë," *Nineteenth-Century Fiction* 20 [1965]: 1–180). Taking a somewhat different perspective, Helence Moglen maintains that the two generations function together to illustrate stages in the development and maturation of the self ("The Double Vision of *Wuthering Heights*: A Clarifying View of Female Development," *The Centennial Review* 15 [1971]: 391–405).

2. Wilson also observes that in addition to reading the novels of the eighteenth and early nineteenth century, Brontë had probably read Scott, Byron, Word-

sworth, Southey, Rousseau, and the Gothic Romance writers of the late eighteenth century—all writers who were interested in the relationship between characters and their environment ("A Personal Response," 234) and thus were less interested in their characters as individuals than as types.

3. Chatman, *Story and Discourse*, 132.

4. Emily Brontë, *Wuthering Heights: An Authoritative Text with Essays in Criticism*, ed. William M. Sale, Jr. (New York: Norton, 1963). Subsequent quotations from this work are cited parenthetically in the text.

5. Miriam Allott, "Wuthering Heights: The Rejection of Heathcliff?," *Essays in Criticism* 8 (1958): 29.

6. Van Ghant, *The English Novel*, 157.

7. *Kenyon Review* 11 (Autumn 1949); reprinted in *Critiques and Essays on Modern Fiction 1920–1951*, edited by John W. Aldridge (New York: Ronald, 1952), 83–98.

8. Van Ghent, *The English Novel*, 157.

9. Jordan, "Ironic Vision," 1–8.

10. Moglen, "Double Vision," 398.

11. John Beverslius, "Love and Self Knowledge," *English* 24 (1975): 77–82.

12. William Madden, "*Wuthering Heights*: The Binding of Passion," *Nineteenth-Century Fiction* 27 (1972): 127–54.

13. David Sonstroem, "*Wuthering Heights* and the Limits of Vision," *PMLA* 86 (1971): 51–62.

14. Arnold Krupat, "The Strangeness of Wuthering Heights," *Nineteenth-Century Fiction* 25 (1970): 269–80.

15. The following table illustrates this remarkable similarity in average sentence length (ASL):

	Catherine	Cathy
ASL of all sentences	14.12	14.7
ASL of all sentences spoken as child	8.045	10.17
ASL of all sentences spoken as a young woman	14.51	15.27
ASL of all sentences when narrating events	26.47	25.14

16. Schorer, "'Analogical Matrix,'" 89–90.

17. The *Oxford English Dictionary* (*OED*) notes the distinction between *should* and *would* as auxiliaries: "The choice between *should* and *would* follows the same rules as that between *shall* and *will* as future auxiliaries, except that *should* must sometimes be avoided on account of liability to be misinterpreted as = 'ought to' (sense 18)," and, in sense 18, "In statements of duty, obligation od propriety (originally, as applicable to hypothetical conditions not regarded as real)." The origin of the distinction is found in the Old English *sceal*, which "while retaining its primary sense, served as tense sign in announcing a future event as fated or divinely decreed. Hence *shall* has always been the auxiliary used, in all persons, for prophetic or oracular announcements of the future, and for solemn assertions of the certainty of a future event."

18. The *OED* explains, "with verbs of liking, preference, etc. *should* in the first person (and interrogatively in the second) is regarded as more correct than *would*, though this is often used."

19. *Will*, and by extension *would*, has traditionally expressed desire as well as intention or purpose and thus its use implies voluntary rather than inevitable ac-

tion. Cathy's choice of the modal *would* indicates her determination to act. The *OED* explains, "In the apodosis of a conditional sentence (expressed or implied), with pers. subject, forming the auxiliary or the periphrastic past subjunctive or so-called 'conditional mood' with implication of intention or volition: = 'should choose or be willing to.'"

20. Randolph Quirk and Sidney Greenbaum, *A Concise Grammar of Contemporary English* (New York: Harcourt Brace Jovanovich, 1973), 201.

21. For a similar reading of Emily Brontë's attitude toward the world as represented by the first generation, see J. Hillis Miller's discussion in *The Disappearance of God* (Cambridge: Harvard University Press, 1963; reprint, [New York: Schoken Books, 1965], 185, 208–211). Miller argues that "Brontë's characters do not hope to escape their situation in life." He does read the second generation quite differently, however, finding them creating a new community, which he calls a new heaven and earth in this world.

22. Allen, *English Novel*, 226.

Chapter 5. Conclusions

1. Robie Macauley and George Lanning, *Technique in Fiction* (New York: Harper & Row, 1964), 53.

2. Ibid., 55.

3. Ibid., 72.

4. Stephen Ullmann, "Style and Personality, *Review* of English Literature 6 (April 1965): 157; reprinted in *Contemporary Essays on Style: Rhetoric, Linguistics, and Criticism*, ed. Glen A. Love and Michael Payne (Glenview, Ill.: Scott, Foresman, 1966).

5. Wetherill also points out that an author may use syntax to illustrate the movement of a character's mind (*The Literary Text*, 32).

6. Friedman, *Form and Meaning*, 102.

7. Muir, *Study of the Novel*, 146.

8. Wellek and Warren, *Theory of Literature*, 418.

Bibliography

Allen, Walter. *The English Novel: A Short Critical History*. New York: E. P. Dutton, 1954.

Allott, Miriam. "Wuthering Heights: The Rejection of Heathcliff?" *Essays in Criticism* 8 (1958): 27–47.

Amos, Arthur. *Time, Space, and Value: The Narrative Structure of the New Arcadia*. London: Associated University Presses, 1977.

Auerbach, Erich. *Mimesis: The Representation of Reality in Western Literature*. Translated by Willard R. Trask. Princeton: Princeton University Press, 1953.

Baker, Ernest A. *The History of the English Novel*, 1. London: H. F. and G. Witherby, 1924.

Beer, Gillian. *Romance*. London: Methuen, 1970.

Bell, Michael Davitt. *The Development of American Romance: The Sacrifice of Relation*. Chicago: University of Chicago Press, 1980.

Benson, Larry D. *Malory's Morte Darthur*. Cambridge: Harvard University Press, 1976.

Bersani, Leo. *A Future for Astyanax: Character and Desire in Literature*. Boston: Little, Brown, 1969.

Beverslius, John. "Love and Self Knowledge," *English* 24 (1975): 77–82.

Borroff, Marie, trans. *Sir Gawin and the Green Knight: A New Verse Translation*. New York: W. W. Norton, 1967.

Brewer, D. S. *The Morte Darthur, Parts Seven and Eight by Sir Thomas Malory*. Evanston, Ill.: Northwestern University Press, 1968.

Brontë, Emily. *Wuthering Heights: An Authoritative Text with Essays in Criticism*. Edited by William M. Sale, Jr. New York: Norton, 1963.

Brooks, Cleanth, and Robert Penn Warren. *Understanding Fiction*. New York: Appleton-Century Crofs, 1943.

Cecil, Lord David. "Emily Brontë and Wuthering Heights." In *Early Victorian Novelists*. London: Bobbs-Merrill, 1935. Reprint. *Wuthering Heights: An Authoritative Text with Essays in Criticism*, edited by William M. Sale, Jr., 287–305. New York: Norton, 1963.

Challis, Lorna. "The Use of Oratory in Sidney's Arcadia." *Studies in Philology* 62 (1965): 561–76.

Chase, Richard. "The Brontës, or Myth Domesticated." In *Forms of Modern Fiction: Essays Collected in Honor of Joseph Warren Beach*, edited by William Van O'Connor, 102–19. Minneapolis: University of Minnesota Press, 1948.

Chatman, Seymour. *Story and Discourse: Narrative Structure in Fiction and Film*. Ithaca: Cornell University Press, 1978.

Clark, Cecily. "*Sir Gawain and the Green Knight: Characterization by Syntax.*" *Essays in Criticism* 16 (1966): 361–74.

Crews, Frederick C. *The Sins of the Fathers.* London: Oxford University Press, 1966.

Danby, John. *Poets on Fortune's Hill.* 1952. Reprint. *Elizabethan and Jacobean Poets: Studies in Sidney, Shakespeare, Beaumont and Fletcher.* London: Faber and Faber, 1965.

Davis, Walter R. *Idea and Act in Elizabethan Fiction.* Princeton: Princeton University Press, 1969.

Docherty, Thomas. *Reading (Absent) Character: Towards a Theory of Characterization in Fiction.* Oxford: Clarendon Press, 1983.

Dolis, John. "Hawthorne's Metonymic Gase: Image and Object." *American Literature* 56 (1984): 362–78.

Donoghue, Denis. "The Other Emily." In *The Brontës: A Collection of Critical Essays,* edited by Ian Gregor, 157–72. Englewood Cliffs, N. J.: Prentice-Hall, 1970.

Duhamel, P. Albert. "Sidney's Arcadia and Elizabethan Rhetoric." *Studies in Philology* 62 (1965): 561–76.

Eagleton, Terry. *Myths of Power: A Marxist Study of the Brontës.* London: Macmillan, 1975.

Elliot, Ralph W. V. *Chaucer's English.* London: Andre Deutsch, 1974.

Feuillerat, Albert, ed. *The Prose Works of Sir Philip Sidney.* Vol. 4. 1912. Reprinted London: Cambridge University Press, 1962.

Field, P. J. C. *Romance and Chronicle: A Study of Malory's Prose Style.* Bloomington: Indiana University Press, 1971.

Forster, E. M. *Aspects of the Novel.* New York: Harcourt, Brace, 1927.

Friedman, Norman. *Form and Meaning in Fiction.* Athens: University of Georgia Press, 1975.

Frow, John. "Spectacle Binding: On Character." *Poetics Today* 7 (1986): 227–50.

Frye, Northrop. *Anatomy of Criticism.* Princeton: Princeton University Press, 1957).

————. *The Secular Scripture: A Study of the Structure of Romance.* Cambridge: Harvard University Press, 1976.

Gerber, John C. "Form and Content in *The Scarlet Letter.*" *New England Quarterly* 17 (1944): 26–28, 29–34.

Gerould, G. H. *The Patterns of English and American Fiction: A History.* New York: Russell and Russell, 1966.

Gilbert, Sandra, and Susan Gubar. *The Madwoman in the Attic: The Woman Writer and the Nineteenth-Century Literary Imagination.* New Haven: Yale University Press, 1979.

Ginsberg, Warren. *The Cast of Character: The Representation of Personality in Ancient and Medieval Literature.* Toronto: University of Toronto Press, 1983.

Greenfield, Thelma N. *The Eye of Judgment: Reading the New Arcadia.* Lewisburg, Pa.: Bucknell University Press, 1982.

Guerin, Winifred. "The Tale of the Death of Arthur." In *Malory's Originality: A Critical Study of Le Morte Darthur,* edited by R. M. Lumiansky, 233–74. Baltimore: The Johns Hopkins Press, 1964.

Harvey, William J. *Character and the Novel.* Ithaca: Cornell University Press, 1965.

Hawthorne, Nathaniel. *The House of Seven Gables.* New York: Washington Square Press, 1970.

———. *The Scarlet Letter.* New York: The New American Library, 1959.

Hochman, Baruch. *Character in Literature.* Ithaca: Cornell University Press, 1985.

Jameson, Frederic. "Magical Narratives: Romance as Genre." *NLH* 7 (1975): 35–163.

Jordan, John E. "The Ironic Vision of Emily Brontë." *Nineteenth-Century Fiction* 20 (1965): 1–18.

Ker, W. P. *Epic and Romance.* 1896, Reprint. London: Macmillan, 1922.

Kettle, Arnold. *An Introduction to the English Novel.* Vol. 1. London: Hutchinson's University Library, 1951.

Kinkead-Weekes, Mark. "The Place of Love in *Jane Eyre* and *Wuthering Heights.*" In *The Brontës: A Collection of Critical Essays,* edited by Ian Gregor, 76–95. Englewood Cliffs, N. J.: Prentice-Hall, 1970.

Krupat, Arnold. "The Strangeness of Wuthering Heights." *Nineteenth-Century Fiction* 25 (1970): 269–80.

Lambert, Mark. *Style and Vision in Le Morte Darthur.* New Haven: Yale University Press, 1975.

Lanham, Richard A. "The Old Arcadia." In *Sidney's Arcadia,* edited by Walter R. Davis and Richard A. Lanham, 183–405. New Haven, Conn: Yale University Press, 1965.

Lanham, Richard. *Motives of Eloquence: Literary Rhetoric in the Renaissance.* New Haven: Yale University Press, 1976.

Leavis, F. R. *The Great Tradition: George Eliot, Henry James, Joseph Conrad.* New York: New York University Press, 1964.

Leavis, Q. D. "A Fresh Approach to Wuthering Heights." In *Lectures in America,* edited by F. R. Leavis and Q. D. Leavis, 83–149. New York: Random House, 1969.

Lindheim, Nancy. *The Structures of Sidney's Arcadia.* Toronto: University of Toronto Press, 1982.

Lubbock, Percy. *The Craft of Fiction.* London: Jonathan Dape, 1921.

Macauley, Robie, and George Lanning. *Technique in Fiction.* New York: Harper & Row, 1964.

Madden, William. "*Wuthering Heights*: The Binding of Passing." *Nineteenth-Century Fiction* 27 (1972): 127–54.

Mahoney, Dhira B. "Narrative Treatment of Name in Malory's *Morte D'Arthur.*" *ELH* 47 (1980): 646–56.

Matthiessen, F. O. *American Renaissance: Art and Expression in the Age of Emerson and Whitman.* London: Oxford University Press, 1941.

Miller, J. Hillis. *The Disappearance of God: Five Nineteenth-Century Writers.* Cambridge: Harvard University Press, 1963. Reprint. New York: Schoken Books, 1965.

Moglen, Helene. "The Double Vision of *Wuthering Heights*: A Clarifying View of Female Development." *The Centennial Review* 15 (1971): 391–405.

Moorman, Charles. *The Book of Kyng Arthur: The Unity of Malory's Morte Darthur.* Lexington: University of Kentucky Press, 1965.

Muir, Edwin. *The Study of the Novel.* London: Hogarth, 1928.

Muscatine, Charles. *Chaucer and the French Tradition.* Berkeley: University of California Press, 1964.

Myrick, Kenneth O. *Sir Philip Sidney as Literary Craftsman*. 2nd ed. Lincoln: University of Nebraska Press, 1965.

Parker, Patricia A. *Inescapable Romance: Studies in the Poetics of a Mode*. Princeton: Princeton University Press, 1979.

Phelan, James. "Character, Progression, and the Mimetic-Didactic Distinction." *Modern Philology* 84 (1987): 282–99.

Porte, Joel. *The Romance in America: Studies in Cooper, Poe, Hawthorne, Melville and James*. Middletown, Conn.: Wesleyan University Press, 1969.

Price, Martin. *Forms of Life: Character and Moral Imagination in the Novel*. New Haven: Yale University Press, 1983.

Pritchett, V. S. "The Implacable, Belligerent People of *Wuthering Heights*, an extract from "Books in General." *The New Statement and Nation*, 22 June 1946. Reprinted in *Wuthering Heights: An Anthology of Criticism*. Compiled by Alastair Everitt. London: Frank Cass, 1967, 152–55.

Pritchett, V. S. *The Living Novel*. New York: Reynal and Hitchcock, 1947.

Quirk, Randolph, and Sidney Greenbaum. *A Concise Grammar of Contemporary English*. New York: Harcourt Brace Jovanovich, 1973.

Reiss, Edmund. *Sir Thomas Malory*. New York: Twayne, 1966.

Roper, Gordon. *The Scarlet Letter and Selected Prose Works*. New York: Farrar, Straus, 1949.

Rudenstine, Neil. *Sidney's Poetic Development*. Cambridge: Harvard University Press, 1967.

Sagar, Keith. "The Originality of *Wuthering Heights*." In *The Art of Emily Brontë*, edited by Anne Smith, 121–59. London: Vision Press, 1976.

Scholes, Robert, and Robert Kellogg. *The Nature of Narrative*. New York: Oxford University Press, 1966.

Schorer, Mark. "Fiction and the 'Analogical Matrix.'" *Kenyon Review* 11 (Autumn 1949). Reprinted. *Critiques and Essays on Modern Fiction 1920–1951*. Edited by John W. Aldridge. New York: Ronald, 1952, 83–98.

Schubert, Leland. *Hawthorne, the Artist*. Chapel Hill: The University of North Carolina Press, 1944.

Schroeder, Peter R. "Hidden Depths: Dialogue and Characterization in Chaucer and Malory." *PMLA* 98 (1983): 374–87.

Sidney, Sir Philip. *The Countesse of Pembrokes Arcadia*. Vol. 1 of *The Prose Works of Sir Philip Sidney*, 4 vols. Edited by Albert Feuillerat. 1912. Reprinted. London: Cambridge University Press, 1962.

Sonstroem, David. "*Wuthering Heights* and the Limits of Vision." *PMLA* 86 (1971): 51–62.

Spark, Muriel, and Derek Stanford. *Emily Brontë: Her Life and Work*. New York: Coward-McCann, 1966.

Stevens, John E. *Medieval Romance: Themes and Approaches*. London: Hutchinson University Library, 1973.

Ullmann, Stephen. "Style and Personality." *Review of English Literature* 6 (April 1965). Reprinted. *Contemporary Essays on Style: Rhetoric, Linguistics, and Criticism*. Edited by Glen A. Love and Michael Payne. Glenview, Ill.: Scott, Foresman, 1966, 156–65.

Van Doren, Mark. *Nathaniel Hawthorne*. New York: William Sloane, 1949.

Van Ghent, Dorothy. *The English Novel: Form and Function.* New York: Rinehart, 1953.

Vinaver, Eugène, ed. *The Works of Sir Thomas Malory.* 2d ed. 3 vols. London:
Oxford University Press, 1967.

Walcutt, Charles. *Man's Changing Mask: Modes and Methods of Characterization
in Fiction.* Minneapolis: University of Minnesota Press, 1966.

Wellek, René, and Austin Warren. *Theory of Literature.* New York: Harcourt,
Brace, 1949.

Wellek, René. "Closing Statement." In *Style in Language,* edited by Thomas A.
Sebeok, 418–27. Cambridge: The MIT Press, 1960.

Wetherill, P. M. *The Literary Text: An Examination of Critical Methods.* Berkeley:
University of California Press, 1974.

Wilson, Colin. "A Personal Response to *Wuthering Heights.*" In *The Art of Emily
Brontë,* edited by Ann Smith, 223–37. London: Vision, 1976.

Wofford, Susanne Lindgren. "Britomart's Petrachan Lament: Allegory and Narrative in *The Fairie Queene* III, iv." *Comparative Literature* 39 (1987): 28–57.

Wright, Thomas. "The Tale of King Arthur: Beginnings and Foreshadowings." In
Malory's Originality: A Critical Study of Le Morte Darthur, edited by R. M.
Lumiansky, 9–66. Baltimore: Johns Hopkins, 1964.

Zandvoort, R. W. *Sidney's 'Arcadia,' A Comparison Between the Two Versions.*
Amsterdam: Swets and Zeitlinger, 1929.

Index